Bennie Kara

GRAHAM NUTHALL'S

HIDDEN LIVES OF LEARNERS IN ACTION

IN ACTION SERIES | EDITOR **TOM SHERRINGTON**

FOREWORD BY ALEX QUIGLEY
OVER ILLUSTRATION BY OLIVER CAVIGLIOLI

A **WALKTHRUs** PRODUCTION

hachette LEARNING

To order, please visit www.HachetteLearning.com or contact Customer Service at education@hachette.co.uk / +44 (0)1235 827827.

ISBN: 978 1 0360 03586

First published in 2025 by
Hachette Learning,
An Hachette UK Company
Carmelite House
50 Victoria Embankment
London EC4Y 0DZ
www.HachetteLearning.com

The authorised representative in the EEA is Hachette Ireland, 8 Castlecourt Centre, Dublin 15, D15 XTP3, Ireland (email: info@hbgi.ie)

Impression 10 9 8 7 6 5 4 3 2 1
Year 2029 2028 2027 2026 2025

A catalogue record for this title is available from the British Library

Cover illustration by Oliver Caviglioli
Illustrations by DC Graphic Design Limited, Hextable, Kent
Typeset in the UK by DC Graphic Design Limited, Hextable, Kent
Printed in the UK by CPI Group.

FOREWORD BY ALEX QUIGLEY

Reading research can too often feel disconnected to their daily experience of busy teachers. Graham Nuthall's *The Hidden Lives of Learners* is such a challenge to that notion because it scrupulously captures the reality of the classroom in a way that it surprises, excites, informs, and even transforms, its reader. I would even argue that reading *The Hidden Lives of Learners* can transform what a teacher or leader thinks about teaching and learning. It did for me.

In a work of teacher hacks, shortcuts and scripts, Nuthall explores the infinite variety of learning and teaching that cannot be pinned down easily into a formula. Instead, he poses the vital importance of a deep understanding of how students learn and the promotion of teacher judgement in the crucible of the classroom.

When I read Nuthall's research for the first time, its distillation of thousands of hours of life in the classroom helped me to crystalise my rationale for my moment-to-moment decisions as a teacher. It posed an explanation for so many of my near-hidden teaching failures, as well as offering evidence-informed principles for teaching better.

Nuthall's research laid the ground for future research, such as Professor Rob Coe's 'poor proxies for learning'. Nuthall's observation that 'students can be busiest and most involved with material they already know', and that 'students already know about 40 to 50 percent of what the teacher is teaching' was a revelation for me as a tired teacher trying his best to do an effective job. It made me think again, and anew, about my teaching, and my students' learning.

The insights gleaned from *Hidden Lives* appear both seminal, rooted in time and place, whilst being endlessly relent to current educational issues. A current interest in adaptive teaching, or supporting students with SEND, is addressed in his close analysis of 'individual differences' and the insight that 'each student experiences the classroom differently, so much so that about a third of what a student learns is unique to that student; it is not learned by other students in the class'.

Like most of *Hidden Lives*, the insight that every student experiences the classroom differently, seems startingly obvious and yet I'd never really considered it so clearly before. What Nuthall does best is offer a language – and quite literally a lens – on the complexities of the classroom, whilst giving us a language to address the challenge.

Another startingly revelation from *Hidden Lives* – that seems so obvious when you think about it – are that there are three separate worlds of the classroom.

There is the conventional ‘public world’ that the teachers see and manage. But then there is the ‘social world’ where students play their part talking to one another and interpreting the lesson and more. Finally, there is the ‘private world’ hidden to teachers where thinking and learning really takes place.

You don’t need to scratch too far into your own memories of school to remember the importance of your classmates to your learning. What my teachers said mattered, but sometimes what my friends said mattered just as much. Nuthall paints this picture with his typical precision to unveil the ‘peer culture that wins every time’!

You are left having read *Hidden Lives* with as many reflections as answers for how to teach better. But the knowledge the research offers us is vital for the reflectiveness and sensitive adaptations to practice that an expert teacher seeks to enact.

Bennie Kara’s *In Action* book is the perfect accompaniment to the research of Nuthall. It further deepens insights and reflections, but it crucially offers more practical explications informed by the original research. The planning and preparation time of teachers is so precious that I don’t take this advice lightly: but use it to read this book.

If you are a leader read, reflect, then build on its insights and get everyone else reading it too. If you are a teacher, enjoy seeing the hidden life you live in the classroom be prostrated with startling clarity and usefulness. And then go make a difference to your students, just like Nuthall wanted.

SERIES FOREWORD BY TOM SHERRINGTON

The idea for the *In Action* series was developed by John Catt's *Teaching WalkThrus* team after we saw how popular our *Rosenshine's Principles in Action* booklets proved to be. We realised that the same approach might support teachers to access the ideas of a range of researchers, cognitive scientists and educators. A constant challenge that we wrestle with in the world of teaching and education research is the significant distance between the formulation of a set of concepts and conclusions that might be useful to teachers and the moment when a teacher uses those ideas to teach their students in a more effective manner, thereby succeeding in securing deeper or richer learning. Sometimes so much meaning is lost along that journey, through all the communication barriers that line the road, that the implementation of the idea bears no relation to the concept its originator had in mind. Sometimes it's more powerful to hear from a teacher about how they implemented an idea than it is to read about the idea from a researcher or cognitive scientist directly – because they reduce that distance; they push some of those barriers aside.

In our *In Action* series, the authors and their collaborative partners are all current or former teachers or school leaders close to the action in classrooms in real schools. Their strategies for translating their subjects' work into practice bring fresh energy to a powerful set of original ideas in a way that we're confident will support teachers with their professional learning and, ultimately, their classroom practice. In doing so, they are also paying their respects to the original researchers and their work. In education, as in so many walks of life, we are standing on the shoulders of giants. We believe that our selection of featured researchers and papers represents some of the most important work done in the field of education in recent times.

In this book, Bennie Kara delivers a fresh and insightful exploration of the classic work *Hidden Lives of Learners* by Graham Nuthall. As Alex Quigley emphasises in his foreword, it's a hugely influential book that is a firm favourite of many teachers and leaders and education commentators – myself included. Given its popularity, it is arguably rather a brave undertaking to apply the *In Action* process to *Hidden Lives*, but, drawing on her extensive experience in classrooms as a teacher and a school leader, Bennie has triumphed!

Hidden Lives of Learners is very wide ranging, bringing together ideas from cognitive science and the empirical research Nuthall and his team undertook over decades. Their process and conclusions are equally fascinating. Bennie has packed her analysis with examples of how Nuthall's ideas can be acted on in practice. I have no doubt that, on reading this book, many teachers will want to read the original book if they haven't already done so. However, from this book alone, readers will be challenged to reconsider numerous assumptions about what learning looks like and how to secure it over the long term given the complex interactions that are ever present in our classrooms.

Finally, in producing this series, we would like to acknowledge the significant influence of the researchED movement that started in 2013. I was present at the first conference and, having seen the movement grow over the intervening years, I feel that many of us, including several *In Action* authors, owe a significant debt of gratitude to researchED for providing the forum where teachers' and researchers' ideas and perspectives can be shared. We are delighted, therefore, to be contributing a share of the royalties to researchED to support them in their ongoing non-profit work.

CONTENTS

INTRODUCTION

It is hard to name researchers in the field of teaching and learning who have served the profession for as long as Graham Nuthall. Nuthall was born in 1935, and went on to become professor of education and teaching research at the University of Canterbury in New Zealand at the age of 37, thus beginning one of the most extensive studies in education history of the link between learners and how they learn. He was awarded the Order of New Zealand for long-standing service to education in 2003, and he died not long after in 2004.

This book is not a mere summary of Nuthall's work in *The Hidden Lives of Learners*. It draws on his research to provide practical, actionable steps to take in the classroom to ensure that long-term learning is at the heart of our practice in education.

Fundamental to Nuthall's work is the need to understand the process of learning outside the constraints of age and stage. In chapter 2, 'The learning process', we aim to demonstrate that it is not useful to assume that a student in Year 9 will know about World War I just because they may have studied it previously. This becomes especially important when considering the transition between the primary phase and the secondary phase, where the gaps in curricular transition can occur. Nuthall poses the idea that students construct meaning in learning based on aspects such as prior learning, their own experiences (lived and imagined) and also, crucially, their interactions in the classroom. It is also problematic to assume levels of understanding from prior test scores, from generalisations about a student's background or from the ways in which they interact in the classroom. Participation is a superficial indicator of understanding. In his work, Professor Rob Coe has referred to this as one of many poor proxies for learning.

Poor proxies for learning

- Students are busy; lots of work is done (especially written work).
- Students are engaged, interested, motivated.
- Students are getting attention, feedback, explanations.
- The classroom is ordered, calm, under control.
- (At least some) Students have supplied correct answers, even if they:
    - Have not really understood them.
    - Could not reproduce them independently.
    - Will have forgotten it by next week/tomorrow.
    - Already knew how to do this anyway.

Source: Professor Rob Coe's (2021) presentation on what makes good teaching, originally shared by Tom Sherrington in 2014.

Nuthall's research tells us that students are profoundly influenced by their individual experiences in the classroom. We will explore this further in chapter 3, 'The role of student experience'. Nuthall poses the theory that students exist in 'three worlds' of experience: one defined by teacher instruction, another defined by social interaction with peers, and the last, the private, inner world of thought and reflection. In order to be effective as a teacher, one must try to loop together these three worlds so that a student's private understanding aligns with the teacher's goals of understanding.

As we explain in chapter 4, 'Frequent and formative feedback', if we are to gauge this understanding, we as teachers must place emphasis on giving ongoing and formative feedback – not in order to measure retention or as a data-collecting exercise, but to constantly assess how students are making sense of the content being taught. In this way, teachers are able to shape feedback effectively. Summative assessment, according to Nuthall, is often relied upon too heavily, and the delay in feedback from summative assessments contributes to poorer learning in the long term.

Nuthall's belief that we should acknowledge and focus on individual learning needs may be subject to misconceptions and certainly does not warrant individualised resourcing in the way that adaptive teaching has seemed to promote in years gone by. If anything, Nuthall proposes that we take care in our use of a variety of instructional strategies, and suggests that one-size-fits-all teaching may not yield the best results for young people in the long term – a view that is expanded upon in chapter 5, 'Focusing on individual student needs'.

To be effective as a teacher, Nuthall keeps coming back to the ways in which teachers both create and capitalise on multiple opportunities for students to learn. This is the basis for chapter 6, 'Maximising learning opportunities', in which we explore how encountering material three or four times and then engaging with it in different ways serves to embed learning in the long term. This means encountering and repeating exposure to teaching material and ensuring that young people can interact with that material in a variety of ways, which gives them the opportunity to maximise their learning potential.

We go on to look at enquiry in chapter 7, 'Creating a classroom culture of enquiry'. The first thing to note is that Nuthall's definition of enquiry is not the same as in discovery-based methods, like those posed by John Dewey and later by Jerome Bruner. Nuthall believes that curiosity, questioning and exploration are key to developing engagement in learning. This requires teachers to build a culture of enquiry in their classrooms that is structured and allows students to express their thoughts about the content they are learning. This may lead to deep engagement with material.

Chapter 8, 'Using data to inform practice', concerns itself with data. Like many others, Nuthall is convinced of the need to collect data in order to learn what students need to do to progress, but he is also aware that numerical data are limited in providing that information. He advocates for the collation of data to include not only formal assessment scores, but also informal observations of student activity within the classroom and student conversation, in the way he did over his 40 years of research. The richness of these data allows teachers to truly understand where students are in their learning and creates opportunities for teachers to adapt their practice more intuitively.

Nuthall is clear that he understands both the benefits and the limitations of direct instruction (DI) – in fact, he deems it necessary, but with caveats. Deep learning, according to Nuthall, is not achievable without the opportunity to make connections, apply concepts and, crucially, discuss ideas in the classroom. As we demonstrate in chapter 9, 'Recognising the limits of methods,' DI should therefore be used as part of a wider toolkit of teaching methodologies, and Nuthall advises teachers to balance this with collaboration and reflection in the classroom to promote deep understanding.

We find ourselves now at chapter 10, 'Ethnicity and learning', which addresses one of Nuthall's key messages about student learning: ethnicity is not inherently a marker of how a student is going to learn in the classroom. He draws on his extensive experience of students from a range of backgrounds in New Zealand, in terms of ethnicity and socioeconomic status. Nuthall's firm belief is that all students, regardless of their ethnicity, will either learn or not learn based on the quality of instruction from the teacher and the ways in which they encounter learning opportunities. In this, Nuthall rejects the belief that intelligence is genetic.

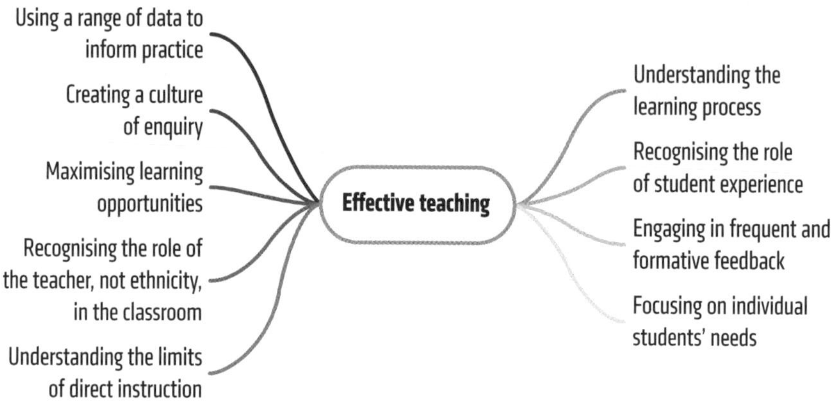

Figure 1: Summary of Nuthall's perspectives on effective teaching.

Takeaways

- Nuthall emphasises that effective teaching adapts to how students truly learn, focusing on their individual experiences and needs.
- He champions evidence-based, flexible teaching practices that offer meaningful feedback and repeated engagement with content.
- He believes that great teachers create a culture of curiosity, reflection and enquiry while navigating the complexities of the classroom.

CHAPTER 1
NUTHALL'S WORK

In 'The cultural myths and realities of teaching and learning' (2001), Nuthall outlines the processes he underwent in examining how effective teaching and learning happens:

Dates	Research Aims and Methods	Findings
1960-1968	Persuaded experienced teachers to let him record their classroom interactions with a tape recorder.	Discovered that teachers followed consistent patterns in their interactions, governed by predictable social structures and conventions.
1968-1974	Investigated beginner teachers to see if teaching patterns could be used in teacher training and whether their methods differed from those of experienced teachers. Worked with Cliff Wright.	Found no significant difference in teaching methods or student outcomes, regardless of whether teachers were new or experienced, trained or untrained.
1974-1980	Collaborated with John Church and David Hughes on experimental studies to measure how teaching impacted student learning.	Concluded that this method was problematic as it risked reducing teaching to a rigid checklist of dos and don'ts.
1974-1980	Conducted a literature review to explore the impact of teaching on learning, with the goal of writing a book.	Struggled with inconsistent research findings and abandoned the project. Realised that teaching is highly individual, making it difficult to create reliable, universal data.
1978-1984	Partnered with PhD student Adrienne Alton-Lee to study three students in detail, tracking every interaction to uncover why some students learn better than others.	Achieved fascinating insights, but the findings were limited by the small sample size. Acknowledged the need for broader, replicable research.
1984-1990	Expanded the research with Alton-Lee to include larger groups of students, extending earlier findings.	Formulated key theories about learning, highlighting the influence of prior knowledge, teachers' lack of awareness of student needs, the impact of peer culture and learning retention.

Dates	Research Aims and Methods	Findings
1995-1998	Studied gender and intelligence to gauge their impact on learning.	Found that more able students have more background knowledge and do more work, but learn in the same way as other students. Challenged the idea of 'academic ability' as an innate trait; the research suggests that ability differences result from how students manage their engagement with the classroom environment. More able students take a more active part in their own learning.
1990 onwards	Critiqued the educational system in which student learning is secondary to management and the appearance of learning, with teachers relying on established routines and rituals.	Highlighted the role of supporting myths, such as the concept of 'academic ability', that justified the status quo, rather than changing the way classrooms are structured. Noted the lack of data on students' learning in the system.

Table 1: The timeline of Nuthall's research.

Nuthall is often seen as a proponent of social constructivism in education, in which we are compelled to trace the ways in which social reality and individual social phenomena are constructed. This concept, originating in the sociological work of Peter L. Berger and Thomas Luckmann and their book *The Social Construction of Reality* (1966), forms the basis of Nuthall's ideas about learning.

The Hidden Lives of Learners (2007)

Graham Nuthall's most famous book is a compilation of the years of his research. *The Hidden Lives of Learners* was published in 2007, posthumously. It is clear from Nuthall's framing of his work that he is keen for it not to be seen as a guidebook for how to teach. He is emphatic in his assertion that there cannot be a recipe for success in the classroom as such, and that his work ought to be seen as a perspective rather than a blueprint, stating: 'it is not possible to just follow a recipe' (Nuthall, 2007, p15).

What is also clear about Nuthall's work is how it straddles the line between qualitative and quantitative methods of analysis of teaching. Nuthall used a range of technology and strategies to record his observations: video, audio, interviews, pre- and post-tests. His work was forensic in its approach to gathering data in its broadest sense. As a result of his use of technology, Nuthall was able to both tap into the personal experience and measure the impact of that experience quantifiably. In doing so, he covered pertinent 'problems' for researchers working across qualitative and quantitative methods, including the perils of transcription and the limits of qualitative work.

Nuthall is aware of the ways in which his work can lead to misconceptions. He points out definitively that his work does not seek to position students from diverse ethnic backgrounds as having different capacities to learn. While he engaged in researching students from a range of backgrounds, including minoritised groups, he did not engage with the idea that there were cultural differences between them in the learning process. It's really important to point out that his research was not an exercise in differentiating students and their learning and attainment according to their nationality or heritage. While he looked at students who came from Afro, American, Polynesian, Pacific Islander and Asian backgrounds, he is very quick to point out in his introduction to *The Hidden Lives of Learners* that he was not studying the differences in their abilities to learn.

Nuthall emphasises that his work is underpinned by excellent research methods, which means that he thinks about it as an empirical activity as opposed to an activity in social interaction. The idea that his work is trustworthy is important to him, and to have credibility it needs to be verifiable, which is why he includes references to social phenomena that have been seen at least three times and thus can be considered reliable.

Nuthall talks about the observation of teaching and learning generally in his first chapter. He explores the idea that observers will 'see' what they plan to see in any given observation, and therefore reward what they deem acceptable according to their individual perspectives. Some people will measure learning by time on task, if they are convinced that this is the only way to ascertain whether learning is taking place; others will see it in the more relational aspects of the classroom, if they believe these to be the true measure of learning. Focusing on the relationship between teacher and students obviously raises some controversies: there is huge debate around whether a student needs to like the teacher in order to learn, or whether that is unnecessary in the classroom. Nuthall points out that judgement of the quality of teaching is therefore largely misplaced. How good a teacher is at promoting student learning must be multidimensional and really focus on – among other observable traits – the time on task and the relational aspects of teaching.

Can a teacher be replaced by a computer?

Nuthall examines the notion that the work of a teacher could be replicated by modern technology. In essence, he doesn't believe that computers, TV or good books can replace the role of a teacher in the classroom, as much as we are living in a world in which artificial intelligence (AI) has started to play a much more prominent role in developing resources and contributing to research in a much more efficient way. He notes that the aspect of a teacher that cannot be replicated by technology is their skill in noticing signs and behaviours that show how a class is responding to what is happening and what is being taught. He references Kounin in 1970, who describes this phenomenon as teachers having 'with-it-ness': they are aware of facial expressions and body language, and this is something that a computer may not be able to replicate. From the way students engage in activities, from looking into the students' eyes, from the quality of their questions and answers, teachers are more likely to be able to see that there is a level of engagement; computers may not notice the subtle human changes in a student's body language that mean they might not be particularly engaged.

Takeaways

- There is no one-size-fits-all approach to teaching and gauging learning.
- Learning is the focus, not the cultural differences between students.
- Teaching is based on recognising nuance and subtlety and cannot be replicated by AI or technology.

CHAPTER 2
THE LEARNING PROCESS

Nuthall makes it clear that learning is an individual and contextual process. He is quick to point out that teachers must not interpret this as a call to identify and cater to learning styles. Catering to learning styles as pedagogy stems from the 1970s, when early versions of learning styles were proposed by David A. Kolb, and later adapted by Peter Honey and Alan Mumford. The most familiar iteration of learning styles is visual, auditory and kinaesthetic, proposed by Walter Burke Barbe (1979) and developed by others later. By the time he wrote *The Hidden Lives of Learners*, Nuthall was well aware that learning styles had been debunked by a range of thinkers, from educational psychologists to prominent educational figures. Nuthall is forthright in his rejection of learning styles when he states: 'There is, as yet, no valid research evidence to suggest adapting classroom teaching to students' learning styles makes any difference to their learning' (Nuthall, 2007, p34).

Instead of focusing on learning styles, Nuthall describes how the following experiences create a student's unique learning fingerprint:

- Their individualised prior knowledge: this might include what they have been taught previously, or not, as the case may be.
- Their lifetime's experiences: this might include their academic, personal, social and familial experiences relating to all aspects of the world.
- The way in which they navigate cognitive frameworks in processing and making sense of information offered to them: this might include the way in which they have learned to handle information over time, based on their prior learning experiences.

The three worlds of the classroom

Nuthall describes how students exist within three worlds in the classroom: the public world of teacher instruction, the social world of peer interaction and the private world of personal experience.

The public world

This is, in Nuthall's words, 'the public world that the teacher sees and manages' (Nuthall, 2007, p84). Students are observed by the teacher following explicit instructions and social interactions, as set by the teacher through a range of pre-designed learning tasks.

In action

A teacher may observe that a student is, on the surface, following instructions and completing activities designed as part of the lesson. But if we only focus on the perception of compliance or non-compliance, we may not have an accurate view of student learning.

The social world

Nuthall describes this as 'the world in which students establish and maintain their social roles' (Nuthall, 2007, p84). This world is acutely important to students, as their perception may be that engaging in this world is just as important as, if not more important than, engaging with the teacher's rules and instructions. This might include post-teaching conversation and interaction, both positive and negative. Nuthall believes that this social world is important in the interpretation and internalisation of learning.

In action

Student talk, both formal and informal, plays a role in learning. Teachers can insist on silence when necessary, but this ignores the way in which learning is compounded through the sharing of ideas (as instructed, or when the teacher is not observing interactions between peers). This compounding may not always be positive, as students can share ideas that are incorrect. Teachers will need to monitor this carefully. If student talk is not present, or is used as the only indicator of learning, there may be inaccuracies in gauging understanding in the long term.

The private world

Nuthall describes this world as one in which students 'grow' and change their beliefs and knowledge, and it may have profound effects on self-belief and attitudes. He states that this is where 'individual thinking and learning takes place' (Nuthall, 2007, p84).

In action

This is the hardest 'world' to gauge because it is highly dependent on the invisible thoughts and perceptions of the student. If we are to tap into this world, skilful use of questioning may be necessary to collate information on how teaching material has been processed. There are many strategies for teachers to help students externalise their personal thoughts:

- Use of mini whiteboards for immediate responses.
- Cold-calling – using a no-hands-up approach.
- Show calling – using a projected piece of work as an example.

- Active circulation and talking with individuals.
- Journalling.
- Exit thoughts – where you capture what has been learned as the students leave the room.

Public World	Social World	Private World
In geography, the teacher designs a task for students to identify and label physical elements of volcanoes. Students complete the task, either correctly or incorrectly.	Students engage in deliberate feedback, recounting answers out loud. There is some laughing at incorrect responses. Students engage in subtle comparison of answers, with some students bullying others for their mistakes. This bullying continues outside the classroom.	A student believes that volcanoes always erupt violently, spewing lava. Their beliefs change after instruction and completion of the task. They initially feel unintelligent after learning they were wrong. They might know that volcanoes come in different varieties and have different physical characteristics. They see a volcano on TV at home and refine their thoughts further.

Table 2: The three worlds of the classroom in action.

Nuthall's assertion that learning is largely invisible because of the way in which students occupy the private world of personal experience means that it can be hard to assess how students are processing the information they encounter. We cannot see a student's cognitive processes, and we cannot know how they have absorbed and assimilated the material into their prior mental models unless there is an activity related to this. Nuthall advocates for having time to reflect on learning, such as through journalling activities or formative conversations in which a window can be opened, potentially, onto what has been understood and what has not.

Accessing the Private World	Possible Actions
Journalling/reflection	An ongoing notebook completed in the classroom; reflection questions on what students knew before, what they know now and how they feel about the material presented.
One-to-one conversation	An informal conversation about what was known previously, how the student feels about the material and what the gaps in their knowledge might be.
Group conversation observed and/or recorded	Allow students to discuss prior knowledge and new knowledge; observe and take notes on their responses.

Table 3: Methods to gauge learning through social interactions and accessing private thoughts.

The need for multiple encounters

Nuthall's research shows that the number of encounters students have with the learning material has a deep impact on long-term learning. He defines 'multiple encounters' as three or four encounters in different contexts. The implication for teachers is that students need repeated exposure to material in different forms in order to embed new learning and make connections to existing mental models. The research shows that identical encounters are not effective for long-term learning; they must vary and might include tasks that involve listening, discussing or applying information in a variety of ways.

Nuthall's research with Adrienne Alton-Lee sheds light on these processes and patterns. From their detailed analysis of conversations between teachers and students, and between the students themselves, it is apparent that a student has to encounter and engage with information at least three times before it is encoded. This is not an arbitrary number. When Alton-Lee presented this analysis, it was initially based on a small group of students. Nuthall insisted that the results be replicated on a larger scale in order to be validated, and this formed the next step of their joint research. They went on to show that the 'three-times rule' was 80-85% accurate in predicting student learning.

In action: science

Two encounters: You explain the requirements for plants to live and grow. Students complete a worksheet filling in the gaps in a paragraph with key terms.

Multiple encounters: You are introducing your class to the requirements of plants for life and growth. You start by pre-teaching language required to access this process. You go on to explain, with a diagram, the requirements of plants for life and growth. You then ask students to analyse, using a worksheet, scenarios for different plants, discussing whether they would survive and grow under particular conditions. Students present their ideas to the class. The teacher provides immediate feedback on responses. Extension of the learning happens via examining which plants might need more or less of the given components and how that relates to their shape, size and structure. Recall activities in other lessons may help to encode the information in long-term memory.

In action: geography

You are teaching students that the wettest place in the world is Mawsynram in India. How will you ensure that this knowledge and its context are fully understood and retained? Here are some possibilities for creating 'encounters' with this knowledge:

- The teacher's introduction references the wettest place on Earth and names it.
- A video explainer outlines Mawsynram's proximity to Bangladesh and the Bay of Bengal.
- The class discusses the wettest places in the UK and the world. (Manchester? Rainforests?)
- Levels of rainfall in different locations are analysed and compared (e.g. Mawsynram's 11,871 mm of annual rainfall versus Cardiff's 1152 mm).
- The class reads a non-fiction extract featuring a resident of Mawsynram.
- Students write an explanation of the difference between Mawsynram's and Cardiff's precipitation rates.

In this example, you can see that there are several 'encounters' with the knowledge and the context of the wettest place on Earth. There are at least three opportunities to engage with the information. Nuthall outlines the need for all the required information to be available to the student in the three encounters, as partial information may not lead to the same success rate.

We must be aware of the potential for lethal mutations of Nuthall's 'three-times rule'. He is quick to point out that just repeating information three times does not equal a meaningful encounter with the information. It has to be 'handled', questioned, applied and evaluated in context. Crucially, in order for the 'three-times rule' to have predictive value, the student needs to have access to what Nuthall calls 'a full set of information'. This is:

- Information that can be seen, heard, read, discussed and used in an activity.
- Background knowledge that students bring to the table and apply.
- Information that is relevant and clear.

Nuthall also defines partial information, and stresses that, in themselves, these partial segments – such as providing terminology, or using activities that do not activate the full set of information – do not allow students to engage with and remember the information fully.

Nuthall also points out that there may be a significant effect on learning if distractions are present. Using examples from his observations, Nuthall 'discounted' encounters in which a student was clearly distracted by activities such as passing notes.

Of course, it cannot be assumed that students have no prior understanding of how plants live and grow. Nuthall's research findings show that many students were already aware of elements of what was being taught. He states: 'Our own research shows that students can be busiest and most involved with material they already know. In most of the classrooms we have studied, each student already knows about 40 to 50 percent of what the teacher is teaching' (Nuthall, 2007, p25).

Nuthall is clear that students might bring previously constructed understanding, or, as the case may be, misunderstanding to the lesson. Their construction of meaning is an active process and they will interpret, filter and integrate new or adjusted information into their mental model. A student might believe that the only thing plants need to survive is water because they have seen their grandparent watering their plants regularly. The new, multiple encounters will expand that knowledge base, adjust their understanding and develop their ability to examine more closely how their grandparent treats each plant.

The role of memory and attention

The multiple encounter process is closely linked to research on how memory and attention impact learning. Nuthall's research shows that teachers need to be aware of how memory works in order to provide the best learning experiences. Working memory and its limitations play a pivotal role in what is learned by a student. The concept of working memory was not defined by Nuthall but by Baddeley and Hitch in 1974. Baddeley's original diagram was far simpler than Nuthall's and underwent significant revisions over the years.

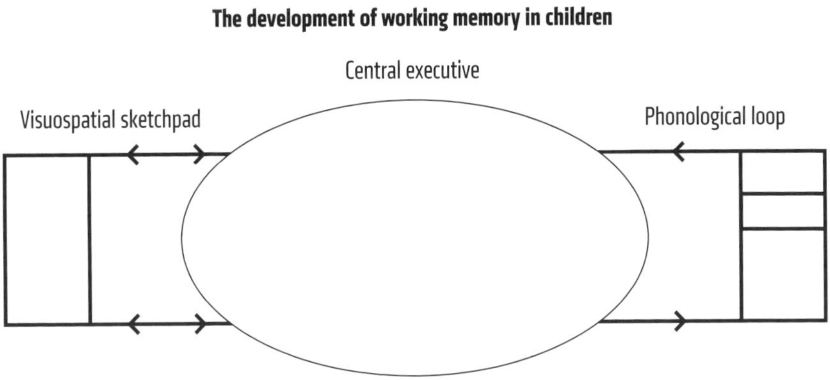

Figure 2: Baddeley and Hitch's (1974) original conceptualisation of the working memory model.

Nuthall's version is adapted from later versions of Baddeley's model.

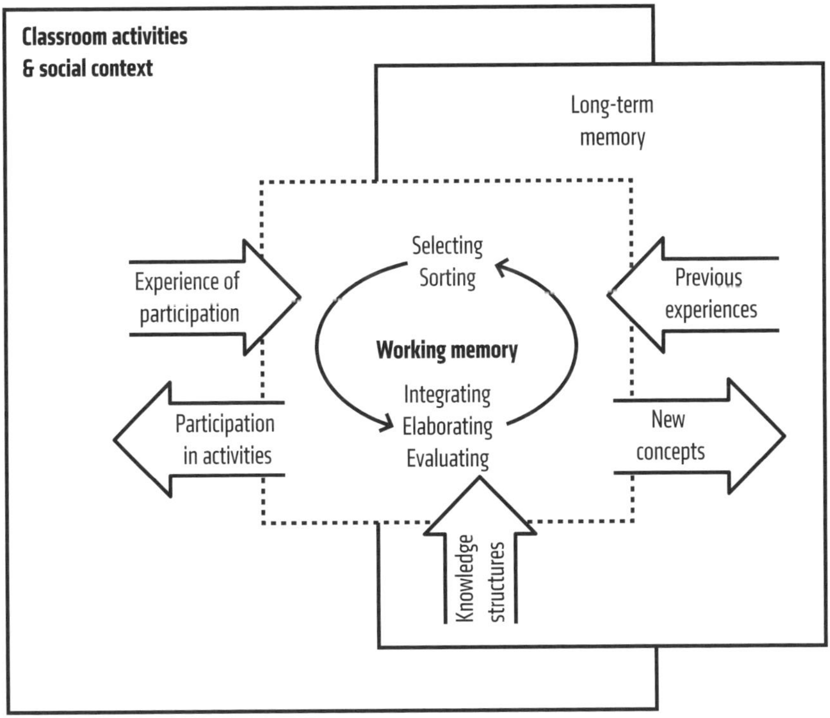

Figure 3: Nuthall's adaptation of Baddeley and Hitch's (1974) working memory model.

It is likely that Nuthall incorporated the concept when noticing what information was held by students, how long they held it and how they used it. In several examples, Nuthall shows that students store information (complete and incomplete) in their working memory and then combine this with previous knowledge in order to learn it. Crucially, he outlines the role of participation and social context in his model. Simply, he believes that learning is impacted by the way students interact with the material and each other in the classroom.

Nuthall's research shows that there could be up to 100 or more concepts introduced in any given topic. If we consider how a student assimilates that information and is able to recall, connect and use it, we become aware that working memory is complex and busy, and that transferring that information to long-term memory requires processing methods.

Expecting variability

Nuthall notes the difficulty of predicting outcomes. As a result of the highly individualised process that occurs when learning is taking place, we cannot accurately know the scope of what is happening. Factors that impact the outcome of a learning sequence might include:

- The prior knowledge of the student.
- Their experiences related to the topic and the language.
- Their attention within the learning sequence.
- Their social interactions during the learning process.

In action: each student has a unique cognitive process

The implication for teaching is clear: teaching has to be individualised to a manageable degree (i.e. without time-consuming gimmicks) and must include encounters that allow the teacher to maximise the potential for deep learning.

Takeaways

- Nuthall emphasises that learning is shaped by individual prior knowledge, experiences and cognitive frameworks. He rejects the concept of learning styles, advocating instead for recognising students' unique 'learning fingerprints'.
- Learning occurs across three worlds: the public world of teacher-led instruction, the social world of peer interactions and the private world of personal reflection. Teachers must address all three to fully support learning.
- Students need at least three varied, meaningful encounters with information to embed it in long-term memory, combining engagement, context and complete information.

CHAPTER 3
THE ROLE OF STUDENT EXPERIENCE

Nuthall argues that the role of student experience is crucial in determining how students will engage with learning. His belief that learning is a personal construct means that we are obliged to engage with several of the realms of experience of young people. We have already explored the three worlds of student experience in the classroom, but how can we explore this further?

Determining prior knowledge

Nuthall recommends that the teacher engage in the process of determining prior knowledge in a culture of openness and trust. Establishing this is vital so that there is no stigma attached to explaining how much or how little a student knows about a particular topic. It might be that a teacher uses a series of tools to explore prior knowledge. The following might be useful, and they require a teacher to observe, listen and record their impressions of the level of knowledge in the room.

In action: diagnostic tests

A diagnostic test might include open-ended questions, such as these when studying history:

- What do you know about castles and why they were built?
- Can you describe what a castle might look like?
- What materials do you think were used to build castles? Why?

A concept map in science might reveal what students do and don't already know. In order to keep learning precise, a teacher might present a concept map about atoms and ask students what they recognise, what is missing and what language is familiar/unfamiliar.

In design and technology, a teacher might lead a discussion based on biomimicry, asking questions such as:

- Why might the human body be a good model of design?
- Which parts of the human arm might be a good model for a machine?

In maths, a teacher might set a short diagnostic quiz to determine prior knowledge of the functions of fractions, asking about basic functions, equivalence and comparison.

In action: informal observation

In French, a teacher observes students undertaking a market activity in which they have to buy food and household items. Students are grouped into fours, with some selling and some buying. The teacher circulates to see which vocabulary is commonly known and which is not. They note down phrases that are commonly used and the things that students struggle to articulate.

In action: use of misconceptions

In drama, the teacher asks students which of the following statements are true and which are false:

- Stages have to be higher than the audience so everyone can see.
- The backstage area is visible to the audience and is used as part of the performance space.
- Arena stages are also called 'theatres in the round' because the audience surrounds the stage completely.

In action: metacognitive reflection

Students could be asked to complete a questionnaire about their prior knowledge, potentially privately to be seen only by the teacher. In politics, this might look like:

- What do you already know about the Houses of Parliament?
- What do you know about the phrase 'separation of powers'?
- What do you know about how laws are made?

It is also possible to use closed quizzes or mini whiteboards to ascertain fact recall, if that is appropriate in the moment. It is important to note that using any of these methods in isolation may not provide teachers with a detailed understanding of the depth of their students' prior knowledge. Using multiple methods is far more effective to create a portfolio of understanding of what is known and what is yet to be learned.

Personal meaning-making

Identifying the ways in which students make meaning is not easy. It is predicated on understanding the ways in which students might develop their knowledge in the moment and over time, and why.

In action: biology and ecosystems

In biology, one student might focus on the scientific names of species because they have a personal interest in biology, while another student might be drawn to the environmental impact of human activity because of their passion for activism.

In action: history and World War II

In history, one student might be interested in architecture and be drawn to the ways in which cities were rebuilt after the Blitz. Another student might have a grandparent who was resident in London during the Blitz and thus be drawn to diary excerpts from those who were there.

In each case, students are engaged in the lesson but draw on different aspects of the learning. In order to gauge personal response, a teacher might want to prepare questions for one-to-one conversations to draw out the personal meaning-making occurring during the lesson. This could happen in the middle of tasks or in conversations with students in groups. The goal here is to draw students from their individual focus to a wider understanding of the work.

The role of ability in learning

We assume that ability will have a large impact on long-term learning, and literature on the subject defines certain aspects of this assumption. In the 1940s, the idea that ability was the biggest indicator of success was already being questioned by researchers. Harris (1940) outlined the idea that non-cognitive factors could add to cognitive ability in order to predict learning – a concept taken on in the work of others who associated the Big Five personality traits with predicting learning. For Harris, persistence was key. For Cattell (1957), it was personality and motivation. Nuthall does not directly cite these scholars, but some of his findings show that ability alone cannot determine learning in the long term.

Nuthall and his team initially paid little attention to ability as defined by prior attainment in the tests issued to students; it was not the most important aspect of the research. However, as the research projects progressed, it became clear that the predictability of learning has very little to do with students' ability levels, as determined by standardised testing.

This is not to say that ability has no impact on learning. It may seem obvious, but Nuthall and his team found that more able students do go on to learn more than their less able counterparts. This was demonstrated by evidence that higher-ability students tend to come to the classroom with more background knowledge. But this wasn't the defining factor affecting learning. Nuthall determined that if all the students had access to the same interactions with the content, then lower-ability students could perform in line with higher-ability students. In short, it was the quality of instruction that made the learning stick.

To illustrate this, let's take a look at the data for five students and compare their experiences:

Student	Background Knowledge	Prior Attainment	Interactions	Actions	Learning?
Lina	High	High	4	On-task talk	Yes
Allen	Low	High	3	Passing notes	Yes
Mai	Middle	Low	2	Off-task conversation, passing notes	No
Sanjeet	Middle	Low	3	On-task talk	Yes
Mason	High	Middle	2	On-task talk	Yes

Table 4: Variability in student learning.

Questions to be asked:

- What factors led to the long-term learning of the different students?
- What role did each of these factors play in committing content to long-term memory?
- How can we recreate this in the classroom?

In these examples, we can see differences in the students' background knowledge, prior attainment, interactions with the content and classroom actions. Take Lina, who has a relatively high amount of background knowledge about the material being taught, high prior attainment in standardised testing, an effective number of interactions with the material and is on task in the social space of the classroom. She can demonstrate that she has started to learn the content being taught. If we look at Mai, she presents differently. She knows less than Lina coming into the room, her prior attainment is low, she has only two significant interactions with the content and she is not academically on task in the room. It is less likely that she has started to encode the content into her long-term memory. She can be contrasted with Sanjeet, who comes into the room with a similar profile but engages better with an optimal number of interactions and transfers the material into long-term memory.

Background knowledge clearly plays a role in learning. Nuthall describes the way in which background knowledge can contribute to learning:

- Different background knowledge will have different effects on learning.
- Background knowledge may or may not have an impact on the way learners approach or complete tasks.
- Background knowledge may also contribute to misconceptions.

More able students are more likely to engage with tasks in a way that is expected, with the notion that they are more accepting of others' ideas and hold more value for academically relevant discussion. What was also noted was the way in which more able students exist in a 'culture' of learning in an academic space, and this may have an impact on their outcomes. Similarly, Nuthall notes that because teachers do not always spend time explaining how to approach and complete a task, lower-ability students are often concerned about the time it takes to complete the task, and what will happen if they finish too early, for example.

This reminds me of research conducted into metacognition. While the earliest references to metacognition exist in the work of Piaget, countless thinkers since have outlined the importance of metacognitive ability in long-term learning. Taylor (1999) points out that 'learners need to become aware of themselves as vibrant self-regulatory organisms who can consistently and deliberately achieve specific goals'. Nuthall refers to 'metacognitive monitoring', explaining that students will make choices about the information they receive – whether it is worthy of engagement, whether they find it easy or difficult – and respond according to these thoughts. In a paper on the role of ability in classroom learning, Nuthall mentions that students will engage in different 'cultures' in the classroom; by this he means the academic or the social, or a combination of both. It is this, he states, that seems to have an effect on long-term learning, not innate ability.

It is also relevant here to mention streaming and/or setting versus mixed-ability classes. This is at times a contentious issue, and Nuthall does not seem to advocate specifically for any of these, but he does reference research on the limitations faced by more able students when mixed with lower-ability students (the language used here reflects Nuthall's terminology). Nuthall emphasises that his data and analysis are not conclusive in this area. He remained curious about the role of ability in the classroom and continued to question its role.

We assume that students will learn more if they complete more activities, but three (or four) engagements with the knowledge will suffice if we recognise that:

- Substantial differences in background knowledge have an impact on learning.
- Peer interactions will have an impact on learning.
- Better metacognitive skills lead to better long-term learning.
- We need to monitor students closely throughout the learning experience.

Social experiences

Studies have shown that peer relationships can have a positive impact on academic achievement. A study of middle school students in China (Shao et al., 2024) reinforces findings by Jacobson (2012) and Gallardo et al. (2016) that demonstrate there is a positive correlation between peer relationships and achievement.

Nuthall's 'second premise' tells us that 'much of what students do in the classroom is determined by their social relationships', and also that 'the student's primary audience is his/her peers' (Nuthall, 2007, p37). We are compelled, then, to engage with the social world of the student and, crucially, to understand what Nuthall calls 'peer culture' in the classroom.

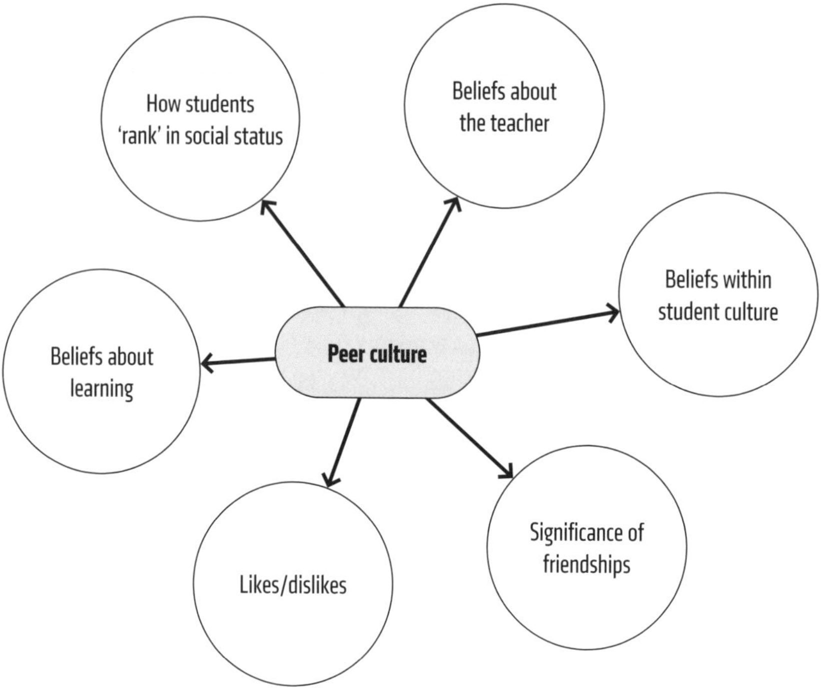

Figure 4: How peer culture appears in the classroom.

So how do we engage with the social lives of our learners? This is not an invitation to 'get down with the kids', but it does present teachers with an opportunity to get to know students personally, to notice their position within the classroom and to engage with students outside the classroom, perhaps on duty in the playground or in the lunch queue. This social engagement allows teachers to see how the student views themselves in the classroom, how much their peer relationships impact their learning and how much their experiences impact what happens during lessons.

In action: what might you notice in the social realm of your classroom?

Student Social Experience	Possible Actions
The student's close peers have a negative view of learning in religious education.	Praise the group for small victories. Link religious education to personal interests. Link religious education to real-world relevance.
The student is socially isolated in English.	Ensure that groupings are appropriate and non-threatening to the student. Have regular check-ins with the student to gauge involvement. Set social 'guidelines' for group work.
A student in your maths lesson has interests in music and drama.	Use examples from music and drama for maths questions. Link mathematical learning to long-term careers in the music industry. Engage in conversation about their interests where appropriate.
A student dislikes the teacher in media.	Have a one-to-one conversation where possible to build the relationship and trust. Praise and encourage the student when work is completed well. Model courtesy and professionalism.

Table 5: Ways to mitigate students' social experiences.

Our role as teachers is much more than just delivering information. By extending our understanding of students' experiences, we can create engaging, vibrant and safe spaces in which students can flourish. Nuthall states: 'there is a need to develop the classroom as a learning community' (Nuthall, 2007, p106), and this brings with it a set of implications:

- The classroom needs to be a safe space.
- There is a need to ensure that social relationships do not derail learning but are harnessed to enhance it.
- 'This is the way we do this here' is important as a mantra, but not at the expense of knowing and adjusting for the individual.

Takeaways

- Nuthall emphasises the importance of determining students' prior knowledge through using diagnostic tools, observations and reflective activities. A combination of methods is needed to build a complete understanding of what students already know and to address misconceptions effectively.

- Students engage with learning differently based on personal interests, background knowledge and social interactions. Teachers must create a safe classroom environment, address peer dynamics and link content to students' interests to foster engagement and long-term learning.
- While ability plays a role, Nuthall's research shows that quality interactions with content, effective instruction, and social and metacognitive factors significantly influence long-term learning outcomes.

CHAPTER 4
FREQUENT AND FORMATIVE FEEDBACK

Nuthall is forthright in his criticisms of summative, test-based assessment strategies in schools. He does not hold back in his view that assessment can become a political football – one that is used to hold teachers to account, rather than to improve outcomes for young people. He claims that 'assessment is an area embedded in myth and misunderstanding' (Nuthall, 2007, p39). In chapter 2 of *The Hidden Lives of Learners*, he outlines these myths and misunderstandings:

- Tests that focus on achievement are primarily tests of motivation and may not reflect what students actually know.
- Test results reported as numbers do not give an accurate view of what has been learned (two students getting the same number of questions right will not know the same things to the same extent).
- Direct recall happens sometimes, but it is rare, mostly because memory works in much more complex ways.

So how do we, as teachers, gain a deeper insight into what is being learned and what the depth of that learning might be? We know that feedback is a core component of learning (Black and Wiliam, 1998). We also know that feedback, in order to be effective, has to be timely and specific (Black and Wiliam, 1998). However, Nuthall is more detailed on the ways in which *formative* assessment relates to a student's experiences of the world and of the learning taking place.

Formatively evaluating learning and prior knowledge

Nuthall argues for greater use of detailed evaluation of learning, as related to a student's experiences.

In action: English

- What a student already knows about the concept being learned: they may have already read some Shakespeare and be aware of aspects of staging. The teacher will have to design activities to gain a whole-class understanding of prior knowledge, such as closed quizzes, open questions or shared discussion.
- Their misconceptions and misunderstandings arising from both private and social experiences: they may have visited the Globe Theatre in London and believe that all stages have a proscenium arch.

- Students' individual differences: the same student might view theatre as a pursuit only for people without disabilities, because they themselves don't have a disability.
- What mistakes are being made: the student might mistakenly present Shakespearean female characters as having been played by women, because that is what they have seen.
- How the students' beliefs change over time: they may alter their understanding if they have access to resources that explain and demonstrate staging, actor casting and costuming with three complete examinations of the concepts.

Of course, in a classroom of 30 students, ascertaining this can seem time-consuming and labour-intensive. In the interviews he conducted with students about their learning, Nuthall posed questions such as:

- How/where did you learn that?
- Do you remember that coming up in our lessons?
- Did you know anything before the unit started?

These questions are designed to uncover hidden learning processes and to probe deeply into the cognitive processes that students undergo during the learning sequence. They are designed to help learning become more visible to the teacher, but they also serve to link learning to a student's individual experiences. There is the added bonus that this form of assessment allows teachers to plan ahead and loop back to concepts if needed.

Maximising feedback opportunities

Time comes at a premium in busy classrooms, so it is worth considering how teachers can maximise feedback opportunities. The Education Endowment Foundation, in their guidance report on teacher feedback, states clearly that: 'Feedback, and particularly some forms of written feedback, continue to take up a large amount of teacher time, limiting the time teachers can give to other tasks and often with a negative impact on their wellbeing' (Quigley and Collin, 2021, p8). It may be worth considering how Nuthall's research sits in the context of your current feedback policy and the impact that policy is having on learning. We might want to explore the ways in which feedback functions in light of Nuthall's research.

Type of Feedback	Positive Considerations	Negative Considerations
Written comments in exercise books	Familiar to teachers, specific.	Time-consuming, can be ignored, delays possible.
Numerical grade	Quick, summative and easily understood by students and parents.	Does not give deep information about learning, a snapshot of a moment, may rest on motivation during assessment.
Verbal feedback	Can engage in a dialogue, can include probing and multilayered questions about knowledge, task approach, change of beliefs.	Time-consuming in lessons, not always possible to speak to every student.
Feedback through technology	Quicker than written feedback, can be sent directly to students through safe channels if recorded verbally.	Technology may not allow for depth of analysis, safeguarding and access issues.

Table 6: Ways to maximise feedback.

With the above suggestions in mind, let us explore the possibilities of verbal feedback in the classroom, where the teacher and student engage in dialogue not just about the work but about the cognitive processes the student might have gone through. We can use the questions that Nuthall's interviewers used, as outlined previously in this chapter. Some of the suggestions below may be possible and desirable, and some may not suit, but we do have options.

In action: grouped observation and feedback

Students complete work during the lesson while the teacher observes, questions and gives feedback to a specific group of students. All students are spoken to on rotation within a given time period, depending on how many lessons you have for your subject.

Example: In religious education, students are grouped to complete an activity on the differences between Dharmic and Abrahamic religions. You observe their work, questioning group consensus and how it is constructed, discussing disagreement and where this comes from, and highlighting misconceptions to redirect group thinking. You provide feedback on group dynamics and effectiveness.

In action: one-to-one feedback

This is a common strategy usually used after a piece of work has been completed and marked. The teacher can call students up one at a time to ask probing questions about their learning, rather than just explaining a mark on a piece of work.

Example: In a maths lesson, you call up a student to complete a task with you using a think-aloud mechanism, whereby the students talks out loud as they solve the equation. You are able to spot misconceptions and provide immediate redirection.

In action: review lessons

Review lessons provide focused time in which teachers can engage in a dialogue about learning. These may occur in the middle or at the end of a unit of work. In this time, students can complete reflections on their learning in writing, while the teacher circulates.

Example: In a photography lesson, you provide journal templates/booklets for students to answer questions about what they have learned about the composition of photographs and how they learned it. While circulating, you read the reflections as they write, and question them to probe the depth of their understanding.

The role of peer feedback

Peer feedback is inherently tricky because it is wrapped up in social relationships. Nuthall relays several instances in which peers can actively derail the learning process or provide incorrect, inaccurate information. It has been said that Nuthall believes '80% of learning comes from peers, but 80% of it is incorrect'; however, there is no evidential source for that statement. What Nuthall does tell us is that students do not know how to provide helpful feedback. The truth of the matter is that the teacher cannot be solely responsible for all feedback in the classroom; we have to teach students to give each other feedback that is impactful and, crucially, allows for social status and relationships to be maintained.

In action

Option	Example
Setting criteria Key stage 3 (KS3) geography	In geography, Alice is unsure whether she has correctly completed the activity on threats to coral reefs. She turns to Samir to check. Samir is able to point her to the criteria and does a quick assessment to answer at least yes or no. Alice learns that she has not described the effects of global warming on coral reefs.
Providing scaffolding for feedback KS2 literacy	In English, Shaun is working with Maddie on writing a description of a haunted house. Maddie is reluctant to share because Shaun has mocked her work. This time, Shaun is told he has to use sentence starters such as 'I can see that you are using ... ' and 'It would be useful for you to ... '. Maddie gives her work to Shaun, who provides better feedback.

Option	Example
Maintaining rules for exchange of feedback KS2 maths	In maths, before students complete a task on angles, the teacher outlines the rules for feedback. They tell the class that they will be observing and listening for respectful engagements, in which the feedback is specific, truthful, helpful and kind. Mali often receives negative feedback couched in insults from his desk partner, Joe, so it is a relief to not have to anticipate this.

Table 7: Maximising peer feedback.

Feedback as an individual interaction

Nuthall recognises that learning is constructed through the three worlds of the student. To do what Nuthall describes as 'shaping learning', teachers might want to consider how individualised feedback can be tailored to the private world of the student. Because each student engages with the material in highly individualised ways, it can seem impossible to provide direction and next steps for each and every one. In this case, there are some possibilities to move us towards feedback that is personal and that taps into their private world:

- Feedback might take into account prior understanding and highlight the changes made throughout the course of learning, or at any given point.

  In action: In a religious education lesson, a student grapples with the concept of original sin and believes initially that God is angry with humans. After studying original sin in detail, the teacher is able to show the student how far they have come in developing their understanding of the concept in Christianity.

- Feedback might take into account personal interests.

  In action: In an art lesson, in conversation with a student who you know is interested in modernism, you might feed back the ways in which the project draws on modernist examples. You might question the artistic choices made according to the project brief.

- Feedback might be formulated as dialogue (fluid and conversational).

  In action: A student has written an essay on climate change but has a poor understanding of the difference between weather and climate. The teacher conducts a one-to-one discussion in which she asks the student about the differences, highlights the misconception, asks a series of questions that allows the student to correct that misconception and uses the dialogue as a jumping-off point for ways to improve the essay.

- Feedback can be used as a metacognitive mirror. Nuthall shows that metacognition is an important tool in shaping learning. Metacognitive feedback can make the learning process visible to the student.

  In action: In a lesson on poetic metre, an English teacher might ask as part of a feedback discussion: 'What helped you determine the metre? What might you do to double-check? What did you notice as you were reading?'

Connections to other experts

Nuthall only refers to feedback twice in *The Hidden Lives of Learners*, but that doesn't mean we should ignore the implications of his research on formative feedback. Both Vygotsky and Nuthall view assessment not as an endpoint but as a dynamic process that informs and shapes learning. While Vygotsky (1978) provides the theoretical framework of the Zone of Proximal Development and the role of scaffolding, Nuthall offers empirical evidence of how these principles play out in real classrooms, emphasising the interplay of feedback, prior knowledge and social interactions in effective learning. In many ways, Nuthall is describing the optimal conditions for shaping learning, in the same way as Hattie does much later in *Visible Learning* (2008). Hattie's references to self-regulatory feedback directly link to Nuthall's beliefs about formative feedback being far better at shaping learning than summative work.

Takeaways

- Feedback and evaluation must occur throughout the learning process, rather than being limited to summative assessments.
- Effective feedback should take diverse forms in order to assess understanding, address misconceptions and engage with the private, social and public worlds of the student.
- Making learning processes visible through metacognitive feedback helps students reflect on their thinking and improve their understanding.

CHAPTER 5
FOCUSING ON INDIVIDUAL STUDENT NEEDS

Nuthall emphasises the importance of focusing on individual student needs as a cornerstone of effective teaching. He believes that truly understanding and addressing these needs requires recognising the unique ways in which each student learns, processes information and experiences the classroom environment. Nuthall argues that focusing on individual needs goes beyond surface-level differentiation and involves understanding the deeper cognitive, social and emotional factors that impact each student's learning.

There are misconceptions to be addressed about focusing on individual student needs. When we consider how many students are in the classroom, it can feel impossible to meet the needs of every single individual, but we cannot allow teachers to go back to the dark days of differentiated, different-coloured worksheets that were handed out subtly to ensure students didn't feel stigmatised by the worksheet they received. Addressing individual student needs is also not about creating thinly sliced curriculum pathways in which students in the same classroom study different things according to their ability or interests. It is worth remembering what inclusion looks like in effective settings.

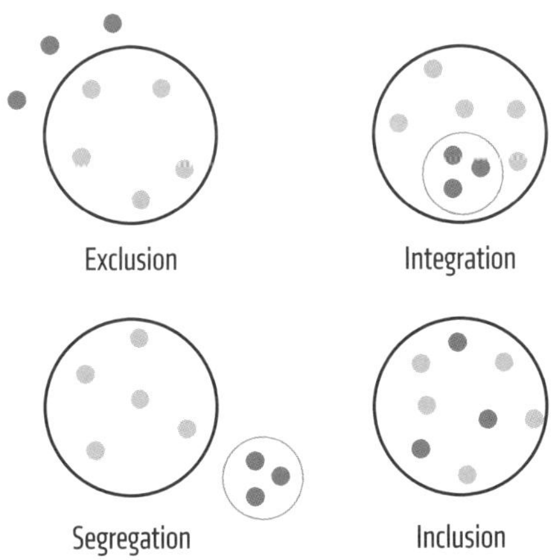

Figure 5: Inclusion model (Engage Education, 2020).

In a 2007 study, Farrell et al. looked at the impact of inclusion in 26 schools. While they found a slightly negative correlation between schools that have a number of students with special educational needs and disabilities and overall attainment, this was statistically insignificant and often could be explained by other factors. What is interesting is how the study affirms Nuthall's emphasis on good teaching as being aware of individual needs. In considering how to cater for such students, the authors found that:

> *... amid the great deal of teaching we saw that struck us as likely to be effective, we saw nothing that was other than 'good practice'. However, we did see how familiar techniques were used to enhance the sorts of flexibility and individual responsiveness that also tended to characterize the structure of provision in these schools. A common feature was that the strategies in use were not inflexible and teachers changed and mixed them to match what they saw as particular students' needs at particular times.*
>
> **Farrell et al. (2007)**

Nuthall believes that the most effective learning environment is one in which the teacher is well aware of the starting points of individual students, and crucially, in which the teacher is constantly observing and recording the ways in which individual students are learning or, as the case may be, not learning. He argues that effective teachers are able to provide multiple entry points for learning. What does this look like in practice?

Creating mental profiles

In action

A teacher of food technology might consider the following before they begin a unit of work on hospitality and catering:

- Has James ever been to a restaurant or hotel setting? This might be something to gauge in conversation or as part of a scoping activity to ascertain prior experiences.
- What is James's experience of customer service?
- Does James have any knowledge of the structures of hospitality settings?
- Does James have any experience of serving food at home?

The responses to these questions would inform activities that encompass the fact that James, and other students, might not have the same social experiences as other students. Students start with different mental models.

It might be helpful for the teacher to complete a mini mental profile of individuals, in terms of not just their academic understanding but the way in which they are accessing learning. Take Pilar, who is struggling to make sense of the different roles and responsibilities in a catering environment. She keeps mixing up concierge and receptionist. As part of a group task on welcoming a very important guest, you might want to give her the role of concierge and give the role of receptionist to another student, with job descriptions outlining each role. In discussions, you can prompt Pilar to advocate for her role and to work out how she functions in relation to other staff. Some questions to ask:

- How many times has Pilar accessed a full set of information about the different roles? If not 3-4 times, in different guises, it may be necessary to consider how that information can be presented to her again differently.
- How has her social environment impacted her ability to commit the information to long-term memory?

In action

In an English lesson, the concept of metaphor is being taught. The teacher has ascertained prior learning and understanding of the way in which metaphors are constructed. There is no assumption that just because metaphors have been taught previously, the students will have a conceptual awareness of their component parts. The teacher provides a clear explanation with dual-coded diagrams and introduces an activity in which there is application of tenor and vehicle; in one-to-one conversations during an activity to identify metaphors, the teacher is able to gauge who is misconceiving the two components and why. In the time the teacher has during one-to-one conversations, they use skilled questioning and allow students to discuss and question alongside them.

Ability settings

Nuthall does not advocate for grouping students into ability settings, in terms of either whole-class or within-class organisation. In order to truly take advantage of the social world of the classroom, in which more learning happens than we have been led to believe, students need to experience conversation and dialogue with others who are both very similar to them and very different. Ability grouping in the classroom makes it easier for the teacher to manage the space and time, but such grouping can be counterproductive as it does not allow for and consider the full range of factors that affect a student's learning, including how motivated they are, how having shared interests with fellow pupils sparks conversation and learning, and how the social dynamics of the space affect understanding.

In action

In a PE lesson, a teacher organises the class into groups of relative ability for a game of cricket. The group that recognises itself as the lower-ability group (for want of a better phrase) may be affected in terms of motivation, and may also be subject to ridicule by the perceived higher-ability groups. Within the lower-ability group, the teacher sees the students as a homogeneous unit. They are perhaps deemed to be less physically able or in need of more time to acquire the skills necessary for proficiency in the sport. However, within that group is one left-handed student, one student who has never played cricket before and one student who struggles to process instructions but is physically strong. It is hard to imagine how the individual differences in this group can be recognised and catered for if the teacher believes them all to be of similar ability and therefore in need of the same level of instruction. They are all asked to practise holding the bat correctly. They are also told that this is the group they will be in until the end of the unit.

What do these students learn about themselves when they are grouped in this way? They may learn that their ability is fixed and that their individual needs are less important than the teacher's needs.

Neurodiversity

While Nuthall did not make explicit reference to neurodivergent students in the classroom, it is important to note that our understanding of neurodiversity has grown since his research was conducted. This section does not have the scope to address all the nuances of working with neurodivergent students, but when we consider that Nuthall was observing and describing the social world of students' experience and processing models, it may be pertinent to look at how that might manifest for students who are neurodivergent. Again, building a mental profile and adapting practice to ensure that neurodivergent students are taken into account is vital.

It is worth asking questions (and speaking to specialists/support staff) about the needs of neurodivergent students. Neurodivergence incorporates a range of learning needs, such as autism, attention deficit hyperactivity disorder, dyslexia, dyscalculia, Tourette's syndrome and dyspraxia. You might want to consider the following:

- In what ways does the student's neurodivergence impact on the private, social and public worlds of the classroom? This might be something you discuss with the learner.
- What strengths does a neurodivergent student have in their learning? This could be determined by the student's own perceptions of their learning, but also through your own observations of their work.
- What mitigating factors can you consider to help neurodivergent students engage in their own way with the three worlds? You can use individual

conversations to map the ways in which the learner feels comfortable in engaging as a starting point.

- How are you ensuring that neurodivergent students are able to process 3-4 full sets of information about a taught topic? Tracking the number of times a learner has accessed full sets of content and monitoring their level of focus on those full sets is another starting point.

Key misconceptions about addressing individual needs

There are several key misconceptions about individualised needs that could arise from Nuthall's recommendations. Nuthall does not address them explicitly in his book, but it is important to know what these misconceptions might look like.

More attention equals more learning

Nuthall tells us that while it is important to spend time with individuals, simply spending more time doing the same things will not necessarily increase student learning. It is the quality and relevance of the interaction that makes the difference. It is far more effective to spend time planning and to use interactions to gauge what the student needs and what they are struggling with, and then adapt your teaching to meet those needs in the classroom. More attention does not always lead to better outcomes, however, so it is important to note that this is not a call to spend no time with individuals and only focus on whole-class teaching.

Only struggling students have individual needs

All students have individual needs. It is a shame that we are encouraged only to see 'need' as something specific to a diagnosis. Individuals' experiences, prior attainment, prior knowledge and the ways in which they process information are unique to them. This often leads to a 'that group will be okay' mentality. Students with high prior attainment may still need careful consideration, as they will have specific experiences both in the classroom and out of it that affect their understanding of a topic.

Individual needs can be addressed by standardised responses

Assumptions about whole-class ability and engagement in the learning process can be deceptive. Generalisations about the needs of a 'top set' or 'lower-ability group' mean that individual needs are erased for all of those students. We can make some guesses about how to pitch a lesson, but that does not mean students will respond in the same way to the same tasks publicly, or indeed socially or privately. If one student has a misconception about reproduction in a science lesson, pitching the lesson lower will not lead to effective learning for them or the other students.

Individual needs mean more resources

It is absolutely clear that the days of differentiated worksheets are long gone. While in some cases paper-based adaptation might be necessary to meet a specific need, it is more effective to consider Nuthall's concept of multiple points of entry as a dynamic and fluid process. Like in the examples given above, in most cases the teacher has considered prior knowledge, attainment, absence, gaps, social relationships and ways of working. All of these can be attended to via skilful questioning and careful adaptation of teaching methods to find ways to 'let the student in'.

Focusing on individual needs slows down the whole class

Knowing the profiles and needs of individuals may lead to greater acceleration of learning because you are spending time ascertaining how students will grasp foundational concepts. By understanding how students engage in learning, privately, socially and publicly, you are able to be more accurate in lesson design and adaptation. Progress slows down when teaching does not consider individual needs, leading to 'one-size-fits-all' teaching that ignores the learning impact of standardised teaching without due regard for how individuals experience the classroom.

Takeaways

- Nuthall emphasises that addressing individual student needs requires recognising the cognitive, social and emotional factors that influence learning. It is not about using rigid differentiation strategies like coloured worksheets or ability grouping, but rather about observing students' learning processes and providing multiple entry points to learning.
- Addressing individual needs does not mean slowing down learning, requiring extra resources or only catering to struggling students. Effective teaching involves adapting strategies dynamically, rather than applying standardised responses or assuming general ability levels.
- Good teaching involves ongoing assessment, questioning and adaptation. Teachers should build mental profiles of students, consider their prior experiences and create flexible approaches to ensure all students engage meaningfully in learning, including neurodivergent learners.

CHAPTER 6
MAXIMISING LEARNING OPPORTUNITIES

Nuthall's research provides significant insights into maximising learning opportunities in the classroom. His work, especially that documented in *The Hidden Lives of Learners*, reveals that learning is a complex, multilayered process that is heavily influenced by the conditions created by both teachers and students. Nuthall's findings emphasise the importance of understanding how learning actually happens, the critical role of having multiple encounters with content, and the need for varied and meaningful interactions to create effective learning environments.

We have already explored the need to encounter learning material at least three or four times in order for learning to be embedded. But how do we know what kinds of activities will lead to the most impactful learning?

From his research, Nuthall was able to identify impactful strategies in the classroom. The profession has moved on from creating lessons that are just an amalgamation of low-impact tasks, such as word searches or gap-fill exercises. Nuthall stresses the need to balance explanation with strategies to embed learning, and highlights that there are strategies that engage learners for maximum impact:

- Teacher-managed activities: These are set by and contributed to by the teacher, and include 'whole class or small group discussion, one-to-one talk with the teacher … or those set by the teacher without student choice (for example, set written activity, required reading)' (Nuthall, 2007, p85).
- Self-generated activities: Nuthall breaks these down into three categories: 1) activities chosen from a list of alternative activities designed by the teacher, like reading, games, writing about a topic, or investigation; 2) activities designed by the students themselves, such as card games to support quizzing and memory; and 3) spontaneous peer talk occurring between individuals and in groups. These are not required but occur alongside activities.

Nuthall shows that students can combine these strategies, and different students rely on different strategies to contribute to their learning. Some learn more from teacher-managed activities, some need more choice and others learn significantly better from spontaneous peer talk.

In action

We can break down an example of teaching healthy eating in a personal, social and health education lesson.

Teacher-Controlled Activity	Choice of Teacher-Designed Activity	Self-Designed Activity	Spontaneous Peer Talk
Reading an article on healthy eating. Explanation of the Eatwell Guide and vocabulary. Watching a video about three students who eat differently. Guided group discussion about which student eats most healthily and why.	Create a video script for a campaign promoting healthy eating for adults. OR Create a video script for a campaign promoting healthy eating for young people.	Healthy eating Top Trumps. Eatwell Guide for your own cultural context.	Occurs throughout.

Table 8: Task choice.

Nuthall's research reveals some interesting findings as to which students rely on each strategy. In one case, it was clear that a more able student relied more on self-generated tasks and peer talk than on teacher-controlled activities in order to learn about a concept. This may be due to a number of factors: his previous experience with the concept, his own familial experiences or his vocabulary knowledge. Nuthall was also quick to point out that some students chose self-generated activities, but lack of completion meant they learned little. The student who had the lowest prior attainment relied mostly on the teacher-controlled tasks. The implication for teachers is that the balance of tasks is important.

Nuthall states that is it important to design activities so that 'students cannot avoid interacting with ... relevant information' (Nuthall, 2007, p79). We have already seen that students need to encounter and engage with information about a concept three or four times. He stressed that 'the ways students understand and interact with information depend on their prior knowledge and understanding' (Nuthall, 2007, p80). As we will see, this cannot depend on prior attainment scores, but instead needs to be predicated on dialogue that creates this awareness in the teacher.

It is clear that Nuthall advocates for active learning rather than passivity in the classroom. In *The Hidden Lives of Learners*, 'active learning' is not defined in terms of concrete activities, but is rather shaped by the need for students to engage with their mental model of the physical and social world in relation to the concepts they are learning. Active learning, for Nuthall, seems to be constructed of private talk, social interactions, engagement in dialogue with the teacher, construction of activities and application of knowledge in different contexts, over time.

Key to this is problem-solving. Because Nuthall tells us 'the single brilliant explanation is not, in itself, enough', we can see that students have to *do* something with the information they receive. How might this happen in an economics lesson?

In action: KS4 economics

In this example lesson, students are introduced to economics as a concept. They learn about economic groups: consumers, producers and the government. Consider the impact on long-term learning of the following approaches.

Approach 1

- The teacher provides a gap-fill task of the key vocabulary.
- Students watch a video on the three basic economic groups and make notes.
- Students individually answer a series of questions on what they have seen.
- The teacher checks their answers to see if they are correct.

Approach 2

- The teacher writes three terms on the board – 'producer', 'consumer' and 'government' – and asks students to jot down if they know what they mean, circulating as students write to check for prior understanding and misconceptions. Students can talk to each other.
- Students are asked to explain what they think the words mean, and the teacher listens and takes notes.
- The teacher provides a brilliant explanation and asks several students how their understanding has changed now. She sees that most students have some understanding of the terms and a few have detailed knowledge.
- The teacher introduces a paired task in which students have to discuss what the relationship between these economic groups might be. She circulates, asking questions such as 'How might one group be reliant on another?' and 'Who needs who more?'
- After this discussion, the class is asked to come to a consensus, with the teacher guiding students away from misconceptions and misunderstandings.
- Students are given a task in which they have to create an island economy, making sure that the three economic groups work together. Students can work in a group. The teacher circulates, asking questions to groups and individuals. Problems are introduced gradually and students have to adapt their responses.

It is clear, according to Nuthall's findings, that approach 2 is more impactful in maximising learning opportunities. In this sequence, the teacher has attempted to ascertain prior knowledge and understanding (even though this example task will not reveal the full extent of it), which allows the teacher to adapt the sequence of learning as necessary. If students have no experience of seeing, hearing or using the key terms, there needs to be a heavier focus on teacher-controlled activities before any problem-solving can take place.

In action: integrating new information

In a KS5 politics lesson, students look at the concepts of power and governance. The teacher asks, 'Who has more power: the king or the prime minister?' The immediate response might be 'the king' because students have prior knowledge that monarchs have power, and they may have studied the Divine Right of Kings in other subjects. When they are given a set of information about the structures of power in the UK, they adjust their mental model. Kings have some power, but less than the prime minister. They might also revise their understanding of how power is conferred. In the same way, in a science lesson, a student might have previously heard that plants need water to grow. If they complete an experiment growing plants under different conditions, they will select and sort the new information from the results of their classroom experience and evaluate their model, potentially coming to understand new concepts such as the impact of light.

The importance of using full sets of information cannot be underestimated. Teachers are often told to 'chunk' information, but this can lead to gaps. Darren Mead tells us in a hugely informative blog post about Nuthall's work:

> *Sadly, this well-intentioned process may not actually benefit student learning; as the most effective teaching activities are often linked to big questions or ideas. This is probably best defined by David Perkins who, in his book 'Making Learning Whole', labels the breaking down of learning into small chunks, rather tongue in cheekly, as a disease, naming it 'elementisis'. The problem with elementisis is that students never get to join the elements back together after they have been broken down for them, so that they may see how the knowledge works as part of a whole.*
>
> **Mead (2018)**

In action: self-generated learning

While the current climate in education may steer teachers away from placing learning in students' hands, Nuthall believes that self-designed or self-generated activities complement the public activities that the teacher designs for the whole class. Nuthall demonstrates this through his analyses that reveal self-generated learning is not a substitute for teacher-designed activities. In exploring this, we need to recognise that the area is ripe for lethal mutations, so we must examine what self-generated tasks could look like in practice and what poor self-generated tasks look like.

Subject/Topic	Ineffective Self-Generated Tasks	Effective Self-Generated Tasks
KS4 history: migration through time	Create a PowerPoint presentation on migration.	Case studies of migrant groups, a local history project on migrant groups, source analysis on how migrants have been represented over time.
KS5 psychology: perception	Write a leaflet about perception.	Design a perception test for how expectations influence perception, find or create optical illusions to explain how they demonstrate perception.
KS4 computer science: systems architecture	Design a poster about central processing units (CPUs).	Research and compare different CPUs based on clock speed, cores and cache size, create a systems infographic on how CPUs work.

Table 9: Self-generated tasks.

In encouraging students to engage with self-generated activities, it is important to keep a close eye on the ways in which the activity will impact the student's mental model, and support their learning over time. It is too easy to allow students to do surface-level activities that do not impact long-term learning. There is a difference between 'design a poster about CPUs' and 'design an infographic explaining how CPUs work for a new audience'. The first may distract the student from engaging with the content of the topic and lead them to focus on non-relevant aspects of the task, such as font and colour, whereas the second requires thought about connections, structures and the skill of explaining something visually. This has implications: we need to teach students how to self-generate effective learning activities.

In action: minimising distractions

It is absolutely evident that Nuthall does not recommend having totally silent classrooms all the time. Talk is vital, but he also believes that distractions can detract from the ability to engage with content meaningfully. For Nuthall, distractions can take the following forms.

Internal

- Misconceptions: In English, believing that all poems with 14 lines are sonnets might lead to misidentification of the form in an essay response on language, structure and form.

- Lack of motivation: In textiles, a student might find it hard to motivate themselves because they perceive that threading a sewing machine is difficult and they do not see the real-life context of the task.

External

- Classroom noise: In design and technology, a student might find it hard to concentrate due to machine noise and off-task noise from other students when they're trying to measure angles for wood-cutting.
- Off-task behaviour: In PE, in paired practice of the crouch start, students push each other over when they try to balance their bodies, out of the teacher's field of vision.

To maximise learning, the teacher has to be aware of how distractions will detract from long-term learning. It might be that they anticipate misconceptions or identify them through dialogue with students. It might be that they are aware of who is struggling with motivation and find a way to link the work to the student's interests. Ensuring that the classroom boundaries are clear and that there is meaningful talk, as opposed to off-task and random talk, are other possibilities. Careful observation of students, even when you are engaged in one-to-one work (e.g. being aware of how talk changes when you are not looking, being aware of where students are and who they are with, being aware of the signs of off-task behaviour), is vital so that distractions can be nipped in the bud quickly and purposefully.

Takeaways

- Structure learning through teacher-led discussions, problem-solving tasks and student-generated activities, ensuring multiple encounters with key content.
- Guide students to create impactful self-generated tasks (e.g. designing an experiment instead of making a simple poster).
- Identify and correct misconceptions early, promote focused peer discussion and ensure classroom talk enhances rather than detracts from learning.

CHAPTER 7
CREATING A CLASSROOM CULTURE OF ENQUIRY

As stated at the start of this book, Nuthall's interest in creating a classroom culture of enquiry does not equate with 'discovery-based learning', although he does recommend elements of self-guided study. How we choose to promote a culture of questioning and conversation is more closely related to Nuthall's research findings. Fostering a culture in which students feel comfortable asking questions and expressing doubts, or even exploring different perspectives, leads to a greater chance of deep learning.

It is important to note that silent classrooms, in which talk is didactic rather than dialogic, may not be conducive to learning if that is the only talk that is allowed. There has been a renewed interest in oracy as a skill since the appointment of Geoff Barton to the chair of the Oracy Education Commission. In the words of Barton (Oracy Education Commission, 2024): 'Dialogic teaching approaches involve teachers extending students' thinking and understanding through talk, enabling them to expose and address misconceptions and gather real-time information on student progress and achievement. It requires skilled teachers who can balance productive dialogue, critical thinking, and respectful interaction across different contexts.' The work of the Oracy Education Commission does not explicitly reference Nuthall's findings, but it is clear that there is a link between *The Hidden Lives of Learners* and the *We Need to Talk* Oracy Education Commission report of 2024.

In action: modelling inquisitiveness

One strand of Nuthall's findings lies in teachers modelling inquisitiveness. This might happen in a variety of ways:

- Verbalising thinking about a topic: A history teacher could say, 'I can see that the caliphs of the Abbasid Caliphate were losing power to the Seljuks by the 11th century in Baghdad. But who was in charge and how do we know? Okay, I have Source A, a secondary source, which tells me a little bit more. I need to make sure that this source is valid and not impacted by later views.'
- Modelling inquisitiveness: 'That's beautifully read, Qasim. I wonder about that phrase "nominal power". It makes me question whether the caliphs had real power.'

- Questioning to make decisions: 'We have two terms here: "nominal" and "de facto". "Nominal" means "in name only", so what does that tell us about the caliphs' level of power? "De facto" means what happens in reality – so does that mean the Seljuks were actually in charge day to day?'

As teachers, in order to develop the notion that curiosity is useful and valuable, we must value all questions as a critical tool of learning. A student might ask: 'So if Mrs Beasely is the nominal head of school, but Mrs Ali does the day-to-day running, does that mean she is the de facto head and has more power?' This question may seem off-topic or even cheeky, but the student is contextualising the language being learned and applying it to a familiar context. The question might need a diplomatic answer, but it is valid as it shows the processing of the concept being learned.

Encouraging students to write questions about content and verbalise them is one way to gauge how critically their minds are engaging with the content. Increasing complexity in the questions would suggest there are multiple layers of knowledge being engaged with, whereas simple factual questions may indicate a more superficial starting point for a student.

In action: promoting dialogue and discussion

Nuthall is clear that classrooms that promote dialogue and discussion, and therefore a culture of enquiry, create more opportunities for students to articulate and clarify their thinking. Classrooms in which dialogue is seen as vital also allow for students to unpick misunderstandings and, crucially, allow them to learn from each other. Consider this example from a biology lesson:

Aaron: So, bacteria are bad for us then?

Teacher: That's a brilliant question. Now that we have the facts about bacteria, I'd like you all to discuss Aaron's question. You have six minutes to talk to your partner. Both of you have to give your point of view, but most importantly you have to use facts to back up your argument.

In this scenario, the debate has been sparked by one student's curiosity or desire to have a misconception cleared up. Using this as a jumping-off point allows students to review their knowledge, weigh up the pros and cons of bacteria, use scientific language and apply their learning.

It might be the case that there isn't a spontaneous question that leads to useful dialogue, in which case a teacher might have to deliberately plan for the interaction to take place. Some ways to encourage diverse viewpoints include:

- Using provocative statements to prompt agreement or disagreement.
- Giving a one-sided view and asking students to consider the alternative.

- Playing 'good cop, bad cop' – making something sound great versus making it sound bad (e.g. 'genetic modification is a wonderful opportunity' versus 'genetic modification is a terrifying example of science gone bad').

Of course, all debate in the classroom has to be predicated on respectful interaction. Nuthall's observations and recordings of peer-to-peer interaction are full of examples of disrespectful engagements. It is important to tap into the social world of student interaction to manage these moments.

Nuthall argues that in a classroom in which questioning and curiosity are central to learning, teachers should not only listen to students actively but also seek to validate student contributions. There is a skill to validation that goes beyond correction and also develops learning beyond the question.

Student Question: 'Is the 2p coin worth more than 20p because the 20p coin is small and the 2p coin is big?'		
Correction	**Validation**	**Development**
'No, that's not correct. The 20p coin is worth more than the 2p coin.'	'That's a really interesting question, Sam. I can see that other people might agree or disagree with you.'	'If something is bigger than something else, does that always mean it is worth more?'

Table 10: Validating responses.

Safety in the classroom plays a huge role in how much a student will engage with learning and how willing they will be to take risks, make mistakes and learn from them. Nuthall's research shows that a safe classroom is one in which all students, regardless of their ability or background, feel they can contribute and express their thoughts and opinions. The research base on psychological safety within a work organisation is extensive (less so when considering the dynamics of a classroom), and it is possible to apply workplace safety concepts to the classroom, allowing for adaptation.

Fostering a safe environment

The concept of psychological safety emerged from the work of Carl Rogers in the 1950s (Vernon, 1970), in which he examined how psychological safety in workers leads to more occurrences of creativity. He stated that there are three factors involved in fostering a safe environment:

1. Accepting someone's unconditional worth.
2. Providing an external, evaluation-free environment.
3. Understanding empathetically.

In the classroom, we can see the importance and apparent simplicity of Rogers' first tenet of recognising and accepting a student's unconditional worth, and yet there is evidence to suggest that unconscious bias still exists in our perceptions of some student groups, based on either their social identity markers or their prior academic performance.

The second tenet is harder to provide as our schooling system culminates in external evaluation in the form of exams. However, we can look at how to minimise the risks of external evaluation by considering where these risks might come from: the teacher and also a student's peers in the room. We minimise these risks by ensuring that we validate and encourage students, as stated previously, and by ensuring that peer feedback and comments are useful, kind and respectful.

The final tenet of Rogers' work is central to a teacher's role in shaping dialogue, in that we are compelled to consider where responses come from, how they might be intended and how they might have been shaped, while maintaining a respectful standard in the room. The essence here is to remove judgement.

It is important, then, to consider what happens when students contribute responses in the classroom. There are distinct possibilities. For example, when a student answers a question incorrectly:

- The teacher corrects without engaging with the error.
- A peer openly mocks the wrong answer.
- A peer privately mocks the wrong answer out of earshot of the teacher.
- A friend provides a sympathetic look.
- Another peer laughs.

It is also important to note the potential reactions when a student answers a question correctly:

- The teacher acknowledges the correct answer and moves on.
- A peer whispers, 'Teacher's pet,' privately.
- Students exchange 'knowing glances' about their classmate's perceived relationship with the teacher.
- Another peer shouts out: 'He cheated!'

In all these cases, the teacher needs to remain connected not just to the public world of the student, but also to the social and private worlds of the student. Creating a safe environment in which to make mistakes, or even to be successful, is vital for developing a classroom climate of enquiry.

Metacognitive monitoring

Part of the journey towards creating an environment in which students feel safe to make mistakes lies in engaging with metacognitive strategies. Nuthall explains that students go through a process called 'metacognitive monitoring' (Nuthall, 2007, p77). In essence, students reflect and make judgements on their learning all the time: deciding whether they know something already, whether a task is easy or hard, or whether they enjoy the topic. As teachers, we should be aware of the possibilities within these thoughts and we should consider how to engage with that mental model. If a student believes a task is hard because they have had previous experience of a similar task, it may be that we need to explicitly engage with how students might think about and approach difficult tasks. Growing a student's awareness of their mental models means they may approach tasks differently than if they have no awareness of their own thought processes. It may be useful to have a set of questions that allow students to reflect on their approach before they start a task, such as:

- Where have you encountered this information before?
- What knowledge do you already have about this topic?
- What are your thoughts about completing this task?
- How will you know if you are successful?

It is tempting to believe that a student has learned something because they have 'completed' the task. Nuthall emphasises the need to monitor the learning process and not just the end product. In *The Hidden Lives of Learners*, he recounts a teaching moment in which a student was learning about refraction. Nuthall observed that her cognitive processes were affected by her social interactions, repetition of language, asking the teacher for help, engaging with her working memory and teacher questioning. This was a much more drawn-out process than simply completing a diagram of the scientific procedure she had used. Nuthall also points out that the learning process continues over time and is revisited, revised and re-engaged with. Creating a culture of enquiry requires recognising the value of the process of enquiry, in which the quality of student questions, depth of exploration and ability to refine thinking are seen as important.

Using collaboration

While Nuthall does not provide a detailed explanation of what effective collaborative work looks like, stating that he would need a whole other book to explore the concept, he does make the reader aware that collaborative activities form part of the learning process. The social world of the student, as we have already seen, is important. It shapes learning constantly. Nuthall explains that students engage in collaboration in ways other than just asking each other questions.

Positive Indicators of Effective Collaboration	Negative Indicators of Effective Collaboration
Comparing their responses to others.	Losing social status through incorrect understanding.
Disagreeing/developing thoughts.	Misdirection by other students' perceived knowledge.
Correcting each other.	Off-task behaviours/irrelevance.
Getting help/not getting help from peers.	Abusive language (uttered out of the teacher's earshot).
Exchanging relevant information.	

Table 11: Indicators of collaboration.

While we can design activities and create a culture that helps to lean a classroom towards the positive indicators of effective collaboration, it is almost impossible to avoid some of the negative ones. This does not mean we should avoid group interactions in our classrooms altogether, but simply that the interaction itself is vital in creating the conditions for enquiry. Teachers can engage with this social world through careful listening, preparation and questioning.

Indeed, it is the flexibility and adaptability of a teacher that are pivotal in fostering a culture of enquiry in the classroom. The ways in which students approach and engage with the concepts they are learning are neither static nor entirely predictable. So does that mean that scripted teaching is ineffective?

There has been much debate about scripted teaching. It is not a new concept; there is evidence that scripted lessons were made available as early as 1888, and of course, in Engelmann's DI model, scripting is essential. However, Nuthall does not comment on scripting, instead choosing to advocate for teachers who can recognise when a student's question is a relevant learning opportunity that provokes deep exploration. There is nothing to suggest this can't happen in a scripted lesson, but Nuthall makes it clear that the enquiry aspect of learning is important and should be front and centre of the learning process.

Takeaways

- Verbalise your own curiosity, encourage questioning and structure discussions that develop students' analytical skills.

- Create a culture of psychological safety in which mistakes are learning moments, and encourage students to challenge ideas, refine their thinking and engage in respectful discussions.
- Enquiry is most impactful when learning is applied to meaningful, real-world problems that allow students to explore, challenge misconceptions and develop critical reasoning.

CHAPTER 8
USING DATA TO INFORM PRACTICE

When we think of data in the classroom, we are often drawn to the numbers that come from summative assessments – those acquired both before a student enters your classroom and while you teach them. Schools, and therefore teachers, have conceived of a multitude of ways to gather data about progress in the classroom. Many years ago, Assessing Pupil Progress grids were a common sight in English lessons, highlighted to within an inch of their lives and often stuck into books, only to eventually be ignored by teachers and the students they were attempting to define. There is still a practice out there that conceives of learning as something that can be captured in the front sheet of an exercise book in a bar chart or list. We have to question who such a sheet is for and how it supports learning in the long term:

- Who is the audience for the progress tracker?
- What does it tell you about a student's learning?
- How does it reveal long-term learning?
- What can it tell you about depth of learning?
- What can it tell you about misconceptions?

It could be argued that an A4 data/progress tracker is just a record of what has been *done*, rather than what has been *learned*.

Another common strategy is to use data to extrapolate a predicted outcome at the end of a stage of education. With the removal of KS3 formal assessment, schools have been left to devise their own structures to provide checkpoints for student outcomes. For example, a student might 'achieve' Grade 4 by the end of KS3 and therefore, if you follow the neatly constructed trajectory, they should achieve Grade 6 by the time they reach Year 11. Of course, this does not take into account the 'squiggly' nature of learning.

It is important to note a very real distinction here, which is made clear by Nuthall: outcomes do not provide a clear view of learning, and predicted outcomes potentially even less so.

Nuthall's concept of data collection goes beyond numbers. In his research, Nuthall collected data through a variety of methods including audio and video, one-to-one and group interviews, observations of young people themselves and the ways in which they engaged with dialogue, and pre- and post-learning tests. Using these methods of data collection, he was attempting to identify the web of learning in the room: how much of it was attributable to teacher action, how much to the public and private interactions between students, and how much to the private world of students and their experiences as learners.

Nuthall's methods in observing and interviewing students provide fascinating insights into how students learn and remember. He makes clear that a series of numbers on an assessment sheet will not provide the kind of quality insight that teachers need to gauge depth of learning. Recording conversations with students and note-taking allow the observer to truly see what pedagogical methods are most impactful in the classroom. It is not necessarily possible to recreate Nuthall's observations, but teachers can adopt the principles of questioning and listening to acquire qualitative data that allow them to plan ahead.

Observing learning through recordings

It might be possible to film your lessons. It used to be the case that schools needed to invest in recording technology to be able to do this, but now it is easy to do using tablets, cameras and cheap microphones. While recording has traditionally been used by observers to gauge the effectiveness of teachers, in this case filming can focus on the ways students engage and communicate. You may not have to do this more than a few times a year to develop a profile of your learners. When you watch the recordings back, listen for questions, misconceptions and completion, but also pay attention to the social dynamics of the classroom. For example, in a media studies lesson, students are using software to design a magazine cover. They've been asked to work in pairs and you have filmed the lesson. Your attention might be drawn to two students, Hassan and Carly, who you know did not complete the task. The purpose of listening to and observing the way they work is to gauge what had the greatest impact on that non-completion and what has to happen next.

Observing one student: interview

Let's consider Yasmin, whose prior attainment data suggest she is broadly average in terms of ability, but in this assessment we can see some immediate flaws. Yasmin has not completed several tasks over the course of the unit of work in sociology. Her assessment marks are poor. If we take these data markers as the only indicators of her learning, we only have a two-dimensional view of how she is functioning and learning in the classroom. It might be worth conducting an interview with her after having recorded the whole class during one particular lesson. In this interview, she may reveal that she feels very uncomfortable with some of the concepts being discussed as she has never openly discussed them before. She has not had the opportunity to rehearse and apply her learning in conversation, and you have witnessed her being very quiet in groups and interactions. It becomes clear that Yasmin worries about speaking about sexuality and feminism because people have criticised her religious beliefs.

Observing one student: group dynamics

To stay with the example of Yasmin, when you look at a recording of a lesson, you notice that the louder, more confident students debate sexuality and feminism, and you also notice that the one time Yasmin responded to an open debate, she was confronted by students who made generalisations about her religion. Yasmin's private world of conflict, combined with the public interactions between her and her peers, do not allow her to fully engage with learning. Yasmin herself doesn't see any conflict between her religion and the concepts being studied, but her perceptions of how her peers see her means she is quieter than she wants to be, and less certain about her responses.

It may not be possible to observe one student's dynamics in the classroom when you are busy teaching a group of 30, but by recording the lesson and focusing not just on your own actions but on the intricate dynamics of students in the room, you may reach a better understanding of why particular students perform well and others perform less well in your lessons.

Keeping notes of your qualitative data

Workload is an ongoing concern in the profession, and it is important to stress here that no teacher can be expected to keep detailed notes about the learning of individual students. However, it could be useful for a teacher to embark on a mini study of some of their students to gauge how the classroom is functioning in terms of learning. How you choose those students might vary and will certainly change according to the needs of school, subject and practitioner. Take a look at these example notes made after a series of Year 10 French lessons and some quick one-to-one interviews:

	One-to-One Interview	Group Observation	Whole-Class Observation
Navneen	Less confident, speaking aloud is a block to learning. Written work feels easier – mistakes not spotted by anyone. Gets confused with irregular verb endings (missed lessons).	Supportive of Damian in the group, who struggles with memory. Gives wrong information twice. Makes notes quickly, speaks rarely.	Responded well to correction on an irregular verb – seemed a bit shy but appreciative. *Pouvoir/dire* more hesitant, moved on through questioning and scaffolding.
Daffyd	Bilingual speaker, loves languages, tries to connect Welsh, English and French. Finds it easy. Doesn't like more complex conjugation, doesn't know which one is which.	Explains Welsh connections to French words to Max very proudly, Max mocks him and Daffyd gets annoyed, refuses to help others complete the task.	Daffyd usually first to respond in whole-class feedback, very quiet this time. Call on him, he has the right answers, even for complex conjugation.
Louise	Best friend is very good and Lou feels uneasy when working in a pair, embarrassed. Misconception French and English have the same sentence rules.	Lou and Parna work with Samir, Samir misdirects, Parna corrects and makes sure Lou has got it. Lou confusing word order.	Lou confident to ask a question about word order, but Samir whispers something to Parna – immediate upset. Lou writes an example I give in her book.

Table 12: Sample notes on students.

With this information, hastily scribbled, the teacher might generate some interesting responses that could inform their next steps in practice:

- Do I need to revisit irregular verbs and more complex conjugation in a different context to give my students another way to understand them?
- How can I celebrate the connections between languages to acknowledge Daffyd's pride?
- What rules do I have for responses when the target language is spoken aloud?
- How can I use display to help memorisation of irregular word endings?

- What homework can I issue to iron out misconceptions?
- What activities can students self-generate to consolidate learning?

In this case, the notes direct the teacher to focus on revisiting key areas of learning, couched in the private, social and public lives of the students. Some might argue that there is no need to keep a physical set of notes, that a skilled teacher can keep this information in their head. While that might be true for some, it might be less so for others. The more pertinent point is: when would a teacher have a moment to take notes like these? I would argue for during the lesson and during the quick interviews, and the teacher can review their notes in planning time.

The teacher might, at this point, review the data gathered from tests. For the purposes of this example, all three students received the same mark on their assessment, which is marked out of 20 and covers a range of taught material from the half-term. The teacher could make the following assumptions from that data:

- All students have learned the same things in this half-term (not true, there are clear variations).
- Some students have specific areas of focus to work on (partially true, would need a discerning teacher to decide how this can be woven into another learning sequence).
- All students are destined to achieve the same learning and outcomes at the end of their learning journey (not true, teachers can make an educated guess about outcomes but not about learning).

Of course, the numerical data give us much less information than the teacher's observations. The teacher is able to home in on the exact issues that create blocks in learning. It could be argued that they could gauge this from correct or incorrect answers, but they would not know from the test that pride, shyness, relationships, social dynamics and masculinity have all played a part in the learning process.

Notes on technology

There are more ways than ever to assess and gather data on young people. The lure of AI looms large over the profession, particularly in terms of its promises around reducing workload. While Nuthall did not ever research or write about the impact (or lack thereof) of AI assessment techniques, we can hold up his principles as a measure of whether AI can truly tell us what young people are learning. While there are clearly real-world applications for AI in the classroom, replacing the capacity for nuance, understanding of social context and the ability to 'read' the room is not, I imagine, something that Nuthall would have encouraged.

Takeaways

- Learning is not linear, and progress trackers alone do not reveal misconceptions or depth of understanding. Use observations, conversations and classroom dynamics to assess learning.
- Brief interviews, lesson recordings and observation notes help to identify barriers (e.g. confidence, peer relationships) that impact student engagement and success.
- AI and automated assessments lack contextual understanding; they can assist, but teachers must interpret the social and emotional factors that influence learning.

CHAPTER 9
RECOGNISING THE LIMITS OF METHODS

Graham Nuthall's research highlighted several important insights about the limits of relying on specific teaching methods, such as entirely constructivist approaches or DI, while acknowledging their role in the classroom. In *The Hidden Lives of Learners*, Nuthall makes it clear that his book is 'not about how to teach' but focuses instead on 'how students experience classroom learning activities' (Nuthall, 2007, p15).

The popularity of DI as a pedagogical tool is evident in the teaching community in the UK, and increasingly beyond. The key levers in DI consist of delivering only 10-15% of new content in any given lesson, and engaging in the practising and reviewing of concepts introduced previously. The instructional design focuses on incremental increase and interleaving, with a focus on individual progress and development. Nuthall would have been aware of the emergence of DI and the research and evidence base that developed as a result. Siegfried Engelmann and Wesley Becker, in the 1960s, designed and refined their approach to DI; the approach has been evaluated in various forms and for various reasons since the 1970s (Stein and Rolf, 2023).

Nuthall was not explicitly critical of DI. However, he had some key concerns about rigid instructional design being used as the only method of teaching. He noted that if passive absorption of content is the only pedagogy used in the classroom, students may lack engagement in learning. Nuthall's concerns lay in the potential for passivity in learning when students are primarily listeners rather than active participants.

Consider the following instructional design of a DI lesson on suffragettes:

<table>
<tr><td>1. Review (5 minutes)</td><td>Recap prior knowledge: 'Who knows what suffrage means?' (Elicit responses.)

Briefly connect to previous learning on democracy and voting rights.</td></tr>
<tr><td>2. Presentation (15 minutes) (Teacher-led explicit teaching)</td><td>Define key terms (suffrage, suffragettes, suffragists, militant versus peaceful protest).

Explain key figures (Emmeline Pankhurst, Christabel Pankhurst, Millicent Fawcett).

Describe major events:

• Formation of the Women's Social and Political Union (1903).

• Protests and hunger strikes.

• The Cat and Mouse Act (1913).

• Emily Davison and the 1913 Derby incident.

• Women's partial suffrage (1918) and full suffrage (1928).

Use visuals (images, short video clips if available) to reinforce understanding.</td></tr>
<tr><td>3. Guided practice (15 minutes) (Teacher-led questioning and worked examples)</td><td>Model a short paragraph on the impact of the suffragettes, demonstrating how to structure a historical explanation.

Ask students targeted questions to check comprehension (e.g. 'Why did the suffragettes turn to militant tactics?' 'How did World War I influence women's suffrage?').</td></tr>
<tr><td>4. Independent practice (15 minutes) (Student-led work with teacher monitoring)</td><td>Task: Students write a short response explaining whether they think militant tactics were necessary for the suffragettes to achieve their goal.

Differentiation: Sentence starters provided for support. Challenge question for higher-ability students: 'Compare the suffragettes and suffragists – who was more effective?'</td></tr>
<tr><td>5. Review & feedback (10 minutes) (Checking for understanding)</td><td>Cold-calling: Select a few students to share their responses.

Summarise key points: 'Let's recap – what were the key events?'

Quick quiz (verbal or written): 3-5 questions to assess understanding.</td></tr>
</table>

Table 13: DI sample lesson.

The concern here might lie in the lack of opportunities for students to engage in meaningful interaction. Apart from the potential for group work in the guided practice phase of DI, there seems to be little in the way of peer-to-peer interaction. This peer-to-peer interaction could take the form of a debate, articulation of opinions and tackling misconceptions together.

DI as part of a sequence of learning

Taking an entirely constructivist approach to learning can also have its limitations. Nuthall's concept of balancing instruction methods means that we can look at how DI and constructivist strategies can be combined to allow effective learning to take place.

Musical Notation	Constructivist Activities	DI Activities
Activities	• Provide students with unfamiliar symbols or visual representations of sound (e.g. graphic scores, pictograms). • Play different notes/rhythms and ask them to associate sounds with their own invented symbols. • In pairs or groups, students design their own way of writing music using symbols, shapes or even drawings. They must include ways to represent pitch, duration and dynamics. • Students perform a short piece using their notation, ensuring others can read and play it.	Clearly explain the key elements of musical notation using direct statements: • Pitch: 'Notes are placed on a five-line staff; higher notes are played at a higher pitch.' • Rhythm: 'Note shapes tell us how long to hold a note – this is called duration.' • Clefs and key signatures: 'The treble clef is for higher-pitched instruments; the bass clef is for lower-pitched instruments.' Use visuals and demonstrations: • Point to notations on a whiteboard or digital screen. • Model reading simple rhythms while clapping. • Play examples to show how notation translates to sound.
Pitfalls	Misconceptions such as: musical notation can be completely free-form, or pitch and rhythm are the same thing.	Lack of deep understanding, limited engagement, limited real-world application.

Table 14: Comparison of pedagogies in music.

So how could a teacher overcome some of the challenges presented in this example? Combining DI and activities that allow students to discuss, challenge and explore leads to a far greater chance of long-term learning. Nuthall is clear that this is a tricky endeavour. He tells us, 'Unless you have a good understanding of how the technique or resource is supposed to affect student learning, your adaptations can only be trial and error' (Nuthall, 2007, p14).

Sample lesson plan on musical notation

Phase 1: provide a structured, teacher-led introduction to notation fundamentals

- The teacher explicitly explains the staff, clefs, note names, rhythms and time signatures (e.g. using a mnemonic device, 'Every Good Boy Deserves Football', for treble clef lines).
- The teacher models reading notation on a whiteboard or interactive screen.
- Guided listening: The teacher plays a short melody while showing notation to connect the symbols to sound.
- Students repeat back key concepts via choral response (e.g. 'A quarter note lasts for?' 'One beat!').

Phase 2: reinforce knowledge through structured, teacher-led activities

- Clap-and-say game: The teacher claps simple rhythms and students repeat. Students say note values aloud while clapping (e.g. 'Ta' for quarter notes, 'Ti-ti' for eighth notes).
- Find-the-note activity: The teacher plays a note on the keyboard. Students point to the correct note on a given staff.
- Mini whiteboard challenge: The teacher gives verbal rhythmic patterns. Students notate them on whiteboards and hold them up for feedback.

Phase 3: allow students to explore notation through creation and problem-solving

- Invent a notation system: In small groups, students create their own way of writing rhythms and pitches. They must include symbols for duration, pitch changes and dynamics.
- Groups exchange their notation systems and try to read/play each other's music.

- Compare to standard notation and have students discuss what worked well in their system, what was difficult to understand and why musicians use a standard notation system.
- The teacher facilitates a whole-class discussion, linking student discoveries to how notation evolved in history.

Phase 4: apply learning by performing music using notation

- Students sight-read a simple melody (the teacher provides sheet music).
- Students play the melody on instruments or clap/sing in rhythm.
- Group work: Students compose a four-bar rhythm using correct notation, then perform it together.
- Self- and peer reflection: 'What helped me understand notation best? What was the biggest challenge?'

This plan is by no means complete and does not account for the multitude of interactions that the teacher will have with individuals. The principle of combining DI and Nuthall's approaches means that foundational knowledge is put in place, but students have the opportunity to experience the classroom in a variety of ways.

Nuthall is cautious about limiting instruction to teacher-led activities. He outlines the ways in which teachers might encounter pitfalls, telling us that:

> *... teachers often prepare materials and use analogies and examples that make new information clear and understandable, only to find students' prior knowledge and/or beliefs lead to new and unique misunderstandings. This situation can be very frustrating and unpredictable unless the teacher has considerable experience in teaching the particular topic or, in other words, 'has seen it all before'.*
>
> **Nuthall (2007, p80)**

He also tells us that the world of the classroom is more complex than the relationship between teacher and student.

Nuthall does not advocate for a particular teaching method, explaining early on in his book that 'in the realities of the classroom, methods do not exist. Every teacher adapts and modifies so-called methods' (Nuthall, 2007, p32). What we can glean from his research is that there need to be sufficient opportunities for meaningful interaction, in which discussion, debate and collaboration with peers are given time, as students will learn from each other as well as the teacher. There cannot solely be an emphasis on teacher control, as this limits students' autonomy and stymies what could be gleaned from self-generated learning: the teacher as sole source of knowledge does not facilitate an environment in which students can learn from different perspectives. Finally, a rigid instruction method may not provide insights into what students are thinking or how they are making sense of new information. It is the role of teachers to reveal these hidden processes through open-ended questions and formative assessment and feedback, and by encouraging metacognitive feedback. In Nuthall's words: 'In my experience, teaching is about sensitivity and adaptation. It is about adjusting to the here-and-now circumstances of particular students. It is about making moment-by-moment decisions as a lesson or activity progresses' (Nuthall, 2007, p15).

Takeaways

- Nuthall emphasises that no single teaching method, whether DI or constructivism, should dominate classroom practice. Instead, effective learning comes from a combination of structured teaching and opportunities for student interaction, discussion and exploration.
- While DI is a widely used and evidence-based method, Nuthall warns against over-reliance on passive learning, whereby students primarily listen rather than actively engage. Lessons must include meaningful interactions, such as debate, problem-solving and peer collaboration, to deepen understanding.
- Learning is not just about delivering content effectively, but also about understanding how students process new information. Nuthall highlights the importance of formative assessment, open-ended questioning and metacognitive reflection to uncover misconceptions and tailor teaching accordingly.

CHAPTER 10
ETHNICITY AND LEARNING

Nuthall makes it clear that cultural, racial and ethnic differences do not adversely affect learning, stating clearly that 'there is no emphasis in this book on ethnic or cultural differences in learning processes'. He goes on to say that 'it is wise to locate the problem in teaching and the culture of teaching rather than in the nature of the student' (Nuthall, 2007, p17).

Race and IQ debates

We would all hope that there aren't still people in our profession who subscribe to the idea that cognitive ability and IQ are determined by race or ethnicity. There certainly was a time when that view was prevalent, but the classification of human beings in that form belongs in the past. However, theories of intelligence as determined or limited by race still do rear their heads. The broad arguments (which are far too complex to delve into here) can be summarised as follows:

- There have been studies, predominantly in the US, that have indicated that IQ is lower in the Black population than in the White population.
- These studies do not take into account that race is a socially constructed entity.
- The tests do not measure the significant difference in social environments and disparities in healthcare, schooling, employment and so on.
- Higher IQs for White and East Asian populations may be affected by their teachers experiencing the Pygmalion effect (i.e. certain students being told they are better makes them score higher).
- Lindsey (2013) tells us: 'What IQ tests measure directly is the test-taker's display of particular cognitive skills: size of vocabulary, degree of reading comprehension, facility with analogies, and so on. Any conclusions about general mental ability are inferences drawn from the test-taker's relative mastery of those various skills.'

A lot of the perspectives on the flawed correlation between race and IQ remind me of Nuthall's view that while the student brings their own experiences to the classroom, which impact their learning trajectory, the social and public worlds of students are incredibly important in learning. Put simply, learning is not inherently determined; it is shaped constantly by many factors.

No two students are alike

The crux of Nuthall's research is that no two students experience learning in the classroom in the same way, so grouping and generalising about the attitudes, experiences and aptitude of students from the same background leads teachers into the same trap as ability grouping. Nuthall's analysis with Māori and Pasifika students is skilfully described, apart from some awkward physical descriptions of the students in question. He outlines their approaches to learning and speculates about their reasoning, but concludes, ultimately, that while they may be influenced by their social environment, their ethnicity does not determine their outcomes. He charts their likes and dislikes, which may be distinct from Western European ones but do not have a significant impact on their learning. Despite the ways in which these students engage with the social environment of the classroom, their learning still depends on the same factors as that of the Western European students, according to Nuthall. He draws similarities and differences between the factors that affect the learning of the Māori and Pasifika students, such as this example from a student named Tui: 'Learning a new concept for him required the same set of experiences as it did for Rata' (Nuthall, 2007, p140). Nuthall was drawn to make the comment because they engaged very differently in the process of learning.

Peer relationships and ethnicity

Nuthall's emphasis on the impact of peer relationships is clear throughout his book. He does take a moment to comment on how ethnicity impacts the ways in which social talk occurs in the classroom. In one case, Teine makes reference to her background with her peers. Nuthall reports: 'So long as she talked about things that were part of their common experience, she seemed an integral part of the social group, but the moment her unique experiences came up, the conversations stopped' (Nuthall, 2007, p146). As teachers, are we aware that talking about prior experiences will be influenced by ethnicity and heritage? Is the classroom a fertile and safe space for everyone to recognise the importance of identity? As teachers, creating psychologically safe classrooms means acknowledging that identity will impact how talk is initiated and received between students.

The curriculum

Nuthall spends very little time commenting on the curriculum as a whole in his book. The very few references to the content of the curriculum appear in his final chapter on ethnicity and learning. In describing Tui, who engaged positively when something was rooted in his interests and prior experiences, Nuthall shows us that carefully curated curriculum choices can pave the way to motivating and engaging students. He states:

> *It seems likely that if the teacher had included Māori concepts related to the weather and the elements, Tui would have been much more interested and involved. This inclusion could possibly have provided the bridge between the culture of the school and the culture of his home and extended family.*
>
> **Nuthall, 2007, p149**

He points out that in Tui's classroom, 'despite a range of ethnic differences in the class, the curriculum did not include any aspects of non-European cultures' (Nuthall, 2007, p149). If prior experience, private interests and knowledge that has been learned outside the classroom are so important in forming a foundation for learning new concepts, then it makes sense that students would thrive in classrooms where the teacher, if not the curriculum, is able to identify this and bring in culturally rich teaching.

In a maths lesson, you might want to consider the following:

Student	Background and Interests	Maths Application
Musa	Pakistani heritage, proud of bilingual status.	Links between mathematical language and Arabic scholars.
Arslan	Turkish heritage, follows Turkish football teams and is vocal about supporting his 'home' team.	Statistics using data from Turkish football teams.
Marsha	Jamaican heritage, admires Jamaican athletes and wants to compete internationally and coach young athletes.	Speed–distance–time using real examples featuring a selection of athletes, including ones that match Marsha's heritage and interests.

Table 15: Engaging with students' interests.

This approach is not to be confused with simply finding ways for students to 'have fun' or to 'make lessons engaging'. Nuthall's work shows us that engagement is based on how we anticipate, adapt and develop the ways in which individuals bring themselves to the table. Their lives, hidden or otherwise, have indelible effects on their learning.

Cultural sensitivity

It is still important to consider how we as teachers can be sensitive to the ways in which culture and ethnicity might affect individuals when they are studying. Topics that are highly sensitive to particular groups of students have to be handled carefully, and it is important to know that these might cause distractions, both private and social, for young people. Where there are tensions between religious views and sexuality in personal, social and health education, where there are cultural norms around bereavement and music, where students are undertaking religious observances while participating in food lessons, it is important to recognise that students will bring these things to the room and they cannot be ignored. While Nuthall's beliefs that race and ethnicity do not impact the learning trajectories of students hold true, it may be worth considering how students' engagement with content will be influenced by their beliefs and upbringing.

The impact of socioeconomic background

Nuthall is also interested in socioeconomics in the classroom. He notes instances in which socioeconomic status might impact a student's experience (note: *not* their learning ability). Going back to Lindsey, we can see that socioeconomics has a greater effect on learning than race:

> *In this regard, consider a pair of French adoption studies that controlled for the socioeconomic status of birth and adoptive parents. They found that being raised by high-SES (socioeconomic status) parents led to an IQ boost of between 12 and 16 points – a huge improvement that testifies to the powerful influence that upbringing can have.*
>
> **Lindsey (2013)**

This is testament to the environment, not genetics, being a determining factor.

Takeaways

- Nuthall emphasises that cultural, racial and ethnic differences do not determine learning outcomes. Instead, teaching methods and the classroom environment play a more significant role in student success.
- While ethnicity does not dictate learning ability, students are more engaged when their cultural backgrounds and personal experiences are reflected in the curriculum. Thoughtful inclusion of diverse perspectives can help to bridge gaps between home and school learning.
- Research shows that socioeconomic status significantly influences educational outcomes, with studies indicating that an enriched environment can boost cognitive ability. This challenges outdated notions that link intelligence to race.

CONCLUSION

Nuthall was meticulous in his research over decades of work with his colleagues, in particular Adrienne Alton-Lee. To truly understand the worlds of learners in our classrooms requires effort, time and energy – all things that can be in short supply in a profession where there are so many pulls on educators' time and attention. This book is not intended to support you to replicate Nuthall's observations in the classroom, but rather seeks to be an overview of the indicators for success in the classroom. The overarching principles of Nuthall's work and findings allow us to reflect on the nature of assessment, pedagogy and the interactions that take place in the classroom.

Nuthall invites us to step away from students' numerical data – not in their entirety, but as the only indicator of a student's long-term learning – and instead encourages us to observe, notice and interact with the young people in our lessons. Nuthall's classroom is not a silent one or one that relies on DI as the sole pedagogical tool; it is one in which every interaction is a learning moment, or at least one that will impact learning in the long term.

In the final chapter of *The Hidden Lives of Learners*, Ian Wilkinson and Richard Anderson provide us with a succinct overview of Nuthall's findings, telling us:

- Learning is highly individual.
- Learning usually involves a progressive change in what a student knows or can do.
- Learning involves extracting information from and making sense of experiences.
- Learning frequently comes from students' self-selected or self-generated experiences.
- Learning of curriculum content inextricably interweaves with the experiences and activities in which the content is encountered, and with the pervasive peer culture.
- Learning is multilayered.

Their thoughts on the multilayered nature of learning in the classroom are captured here in their adaptation of Oser and Baeriswyl's work:

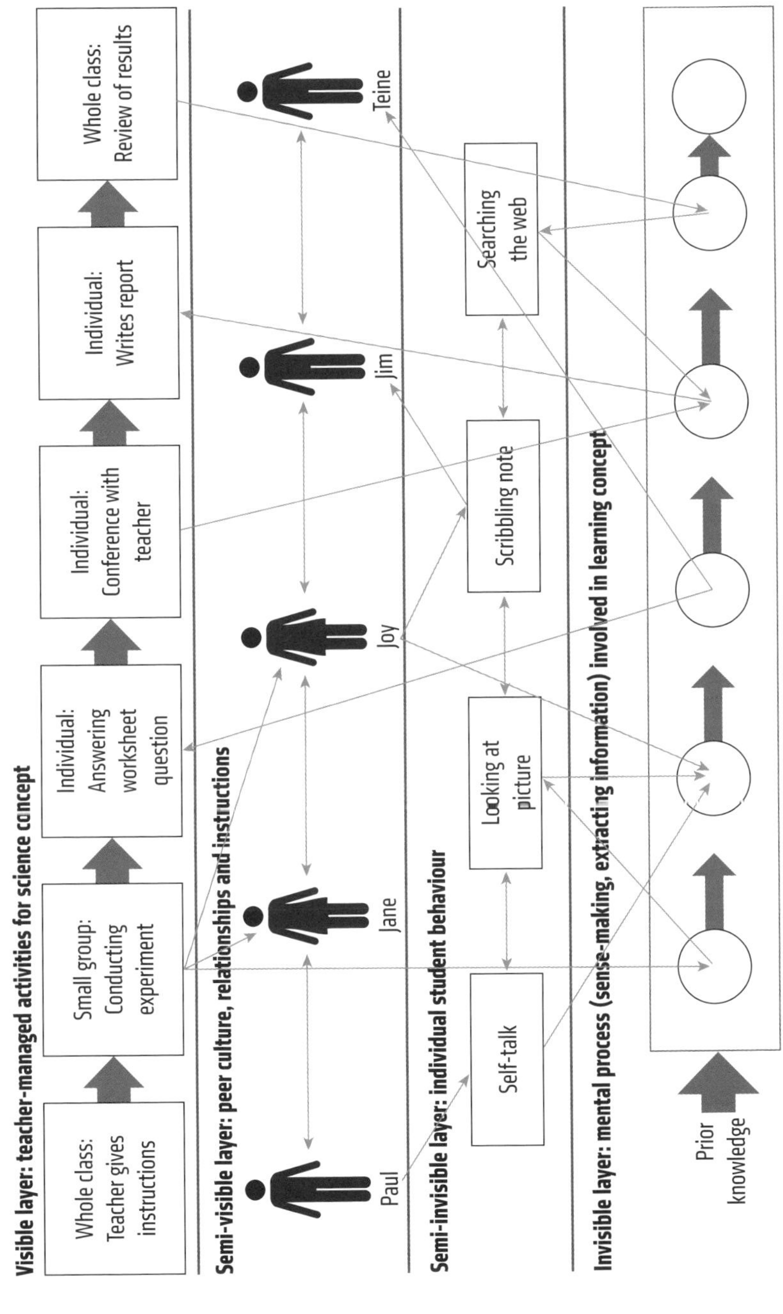

Figure 6: Oser and Baeriswyl's Map of Learning, created by Ian Wilkinson and Richard Anderson, drawing on Nuthall's description (Nuthall, 2007, p159).

On first glance, the diagram is convoluted and requires a bit of mental effort to discern how learning takes place in the classroom. But that is the very point of Nuthall's work: learning is not simple, not always visible and includes processes that happen simultaneously, overlapping and connecting in a multitude of ways.

The beauty of Nuthall's research is the way in which it cuts across binary approaches to education. His research shows that learning, progress and long-term memory do not rely on single methods pitched against each other, but rather that the frequency of encountering full sets of content, revisiting that content and allowing it to percolate in discussions with the teacher and between peers all make a difference to learning. He reveals that while peer culture is pervasive, teachers can create cultures of learning that take into account how this works and its impact.

We will never know how Nuthall intended to finish his book. We will never know how his research might have developed further. What we do have is Nuthall's legacy of enquiry, a deep curiosity about how learners might learn and an appreciation of their complexity. If we take away anything from his work, it is that – alongside deep gratitude for the work he undertook.

BIBLIOGRAPHY

Baddeley, A. D. and Hitch, G. J. (1974). Working memory. In: G. A. Bower (ed.) *The Psychology of Learning and Motivation*, vol. 8, 47-89. New York: Academic Press.

Barbe, W. B., Swassing, R. H. and Milone, M. N. (1979). *Teaching through Modality Strengths: Concepts and Practices*. Columbus, Ohio: Zaner-Bloser.

Berger, P. L. and Luckmann, T. (1966). *The Social Construction of Reality: A Treatise in the Sociology of Knowledge*. New York: Open Road Media.

Black, P. and Wiliam, D. (1998). *Inside the Black Box: Raising Standards through Classroom Assessment*. Cheltenham, Victoria: Hawker Brownlow Education.

Cattell, R. B. (1957). *Personality and Motivation Structure and Measurement*. New York: World Book.

Coe, R. (2021). *Poor proxies for learning. Powerful insights from Prof Coe*. Available at: https://teacherhead.com/2021/07/12/poor-proxies-for-learning-powerful-insights-from-prof-coe/. (Accessed: 4 April 2024).

Engage Education. (2020). *Top tips to help teachers create a more inclusive classroom*. Available at: https://engage-education.com/can/blog/top-tips-to-help-teachers-create-a-more-inclusive-classroom/. (Accessed: 12 December 2024).

Farrell, P., Dyson, A., Polat, F., Hutcheson, G. and Gallannaugh, F. (2007). Inclusion and achievement in mainstream schools. *European Journal of Special Needs Education*, 22(2), 131-145. https://doi.org/10.1080/08856250701267808.

Gallardo, L. O., Barrasa, A. and Guevara-Viejo, F. (2016). Positive peer relationships and academic achievement across early and midadolescence. *Social Behavior and Personality: An International Journal*, 44(10), 1637-1648. https://doi.org/10.2224/sbp.2016.44.10.1637.

Harris, D. (1940). Factors affecting college grades: a review of the literature, 1930–1937. *Psychological Bulletin*, 37(3), 125-166. https://doi.org/10.1037/h0055365.

Hattie, J. (2008). *Visible Learning: A Synthesis of over 800 Meta-Analyses Relating to Achievement*. London: Routledge.

Jacobson, L. T. and Burdsal, C. A. (2012). Academic performance in middle school: friendship Influences. *Global Journal of Community Psychology Practice*, 2(3). https://doi.org/10.7728/0203201206.

Kounin, J. S. (1970). *Discipline and Group Management in Classrooms*. New York: Holt, Rinehart and Winston.

Lindsey, B. (2013). *Why people keep misunderstanding the 'connection' between race and IQ*. Available at: https://www.cato.org/commentary/why-people-keep-misunderstanding-connection-between-race-iq. (Accessed: 2 February 2025).

Mead, D. (2018). *What does Nuthall really say about multiple exposures?* Available at: http://pedagogicalpurposes.blogspot.com/2018/06/what-does-nuthall-really-say-about.html. (Accessed: 1 February 2024).

Nuthall, G. (1996). *What role does ability play in classroom learning?* Paper presented at the Meeting of the New Zealand Association for Research in Education (Nelson, New Zealand, December 1996). Available at: https://files.eric.ed.gov/fulltext/ED414042.pdf. (Accessed: 3 February 2025).

Nuthall, G. (2001). The cultural myths and the realities of teaching and learning. *The New Zealand Annual Review of Education*, 11, 5-30. https://doi.org/10.26686/nzaroe.v0i11.1414.

Nuthall, G. (2007). *The Hidden Lives of Learners*. Wellington: New Zealand Council for Educational Research.

Nuthall, G. and Alton-Lee, A. (1995). Assessing classroom learning: how students use their knowledge and experience to answer classroom achievement test questions in science and social studies. *American Educational Research Journal*, 32(1), 185-223. https://doi.org/10.2307/1163218.

Oracy Education Commission. (2024). *We Need to Talk: The Report of the Commission on the Future of Oracy Education in England*. Available at: https://oracyeducationcommission.co.uk/wp-content/uploads/2024/10/We-need-to-talk-2024.pdf. (Accessed: 1 February 2025).

Quigley, A. and Collin, J. (2021). *Teacher Feedback to Improve Pupil Learning Guidance Report*. Education Endowment Foundation. Available at: https://d2tic4wvo1iusb.cloudfront.net/production/eef-guidance-reports/feedback/Teacher_Feedback_to_Improve_Pupil_Learning.pdf?v=1730293409. (Accessed: 30 October 2024).

Shao, Y., Kang, S., Lu, Q., Zhang, C. and Li, R. (2024). How peer relationships affect academic achievement among junior high school students: the chain mediating roles of learning motivation and learning engagement. *BMC Psychology*, 12(1). https://doi.org/10.1186/s40359-024-01780-z.

Stein, M. and Rolf, K. R. (2023). The case for direct instruction. *Impact*, 19, 14-16.

Taylor, S. (1999). Better learning through better thinking: developing students' metacognitive abilities. *Journal of College Reading and Learning,* 30(1), 34-45. https://doi.org/10.1080/10790195.1999.10850084.

Vernon, P. E. (ed.). (1970). *Creativity: Selected Readings.* Harmondsworth: Penguin.

Vygotsky, L. S. (1978). *Mind in Society: The Development of Higher Psychological Processes.* Cambridge, MA: Harvard University Press.